"Burt Kennedy is the best damn Western director going."
—Ernest Borgnine

"Burt Kennedy writes Broadway in Arizona."
—John Wayne

"Burt has the best sense of humor in Hollywood."
—Frank Sinatra

"A very talented director."
—Kirk Douglas

"Burt had no formal theater training. He just did it."
—Henry Fonda

"Burt is Numero Uno."
—Jack Elam

"Burt *does* what others try to do."
—Harry Morgan

"One of his greatest achievements, from my point of view, is that he showed us how funny evil-eyed Jack Elam could really be when a director turned him loose."
—Elmer Kelton

Hollywood Trail Boss

Behind the Scenes of the

Wild, Wild Western

BURT KENNEDY

BOULEVARD BOOKS, NEW YORK

Contents

This Work Is Dedicated to
Nancy, Amy, Tommy, Gertie, Jack, and Harleigh.
And to Bridget and Susan.

Foreword
by Jack Elam

I haven't seen one line of this book; therefore, this foreword is on the author, my friend Burt Kennedy, whom I have been reading and observing in some detail for about thirty years. His delineations on people and situations are keen and amusing and must make scintillating reading.

I've been told that you're going to read a good deal about some of the heroes, heroines, and heavies that you have been watching for many years. Well, forget gossip columns, forget rumors, forget tabloids. If you read it in Burt's book you can take it to the bank. Walter Brennan said to me one time on the set of Burt's *Support Your Local Sheriff!*, "I like working for this kid—he's sharp!" Brennan was my hero, so who am I to disagree?

A decorated cavalry captain in World War II, Burt's slant on things is from a wide base of experience. His door into the film industry was first as a writer, then as a director-producer. I frankly believe he acts as producer on the pictures he directs so there won't be another producer on the set. The motion picture business is a rude, complex industry, crammed with bloated egos whose only salvation is massage. Burt stands tall among the very few directors who are not of that ilk. Unburdened with a need for power and equipped with a sense of humor, he takes situations and people (including himself) with a grain of salt.

On the set I could always go to him with any ideas I had for changes in the scene or dialogue. He'd listen intently, then we'd do it *his* way. I didn't mind because at least I got heard and knew that if ever I was right, we'd do it *my* way. It doesn't bother me that he's brighter and wittier and richer than I am—as long as he keeps me working.

Some directors, secure in their own right, don't need the satisfaction of "cracking the whip" over the set. They maintain a very pleasant working atmosphere and with these men it's a pleasure to go to work and bust your ass to get it right. If the script calls for distress or pain, they trust the actor to portray it. They don't feel it's necessary to inflict distress and pain in order to capture it on film. Burt Kennedy, Howard Hawks, Sam Peckinpah, King Vidor, to name a few, are artists who indulged themselves in creating "movie magic."

An evening with Burt talking about pictures, people, and Hollywood is a gourmet deluxe. A book by him promises the same pleasures. Due to impaired vision, I wait for the large-print edition before I read a book. This one I'll read anyway I can get it! (At least through the foreword).

Acknowledgments

I want to thank Gary Goldstein. Without his encouragement and editorial expertise, this book would never have made it to print. I also want to thank my "right-hand gal," Nancy Pendleton, and my typist, Harriet "Magic Fingers" Bara. I am grateful to all of the great actors, cameramen, and crews I have had the honor to work with all these years.

Burt Kennedy

Hollywood Trail Boss

Introduction:
Who the Hell Is
Burt Kennedy?

Years ago I did a movie called *The War Wagon,* and some friends of mine in Grove, Oklahoma, population five hundred, asked me if I would bring the film there and have what amounted to a premiere.

I agreed. I grabbed a print of the picture and with my two young daughters, Bridget and Susan, went to Grove, Oklahoma, and ran this picture. All five hundred locals were in their one and only theater. They liked the picture, and when it was over they had me come up onstage and sign autographs.

When everybody had gone home, my seven-year-old daughter Bridget came up to me and she said, "Dad, how come you're famous out in the country and nobody knows you in town?" So maybe I should give some explanation as to how I got here and what I've done.

✿　✿　✿　✿　✿

I arrived in Los Angeles in December of 1946. I had enrolled in the Pasadena Playhouse, which was quite a famous acting school. I had no intention of acting, and I didn't really have any plan, except I knew I was drawn to the business, having been born in a trunk—my folks were a "next-to-closing act" in vaudeville for many years. I was five years old when I went on the stage. I used to sing and tell jokes.

I actually grew up on the stage, so Hollywood was a magnet drawing me to it. I had no reason to believe that I was going to be an actor. I saw *Gone with the Wind* in '39 and fell in love with the picture business.

The war over, I enrolled into the Pasadena Playhouse, and took regular college courses of Shakespeare, Ibsen—all the classics. We also had classes in all the theater arts. I spent two years at the Playhouse. They used to have a number of small theaters, and what they called the main stage. It was a community theater. Seldom were any students allowed to perform—you could *read* for the main stage productions, but it was just a formality.

I read for a play, and I didn't get the part, but the director of that play, George Phelps, said, "The next time I do a show, I want you to be in it."

The next show he did, which was about six months later, was a play called *Man Bites Dog*. It was by Sam and Bella Spewack. Kirk Douglas did it on Broadway.

They cast me as the young lieutenant in the piece. George Reeves, the first Superman, who died tragically, was in the play. We did it, and I was completely at home onstage and got a lot of laughs. But I made an enemy. The dean of the Playhouse—his name was John Brown Henry, I think, or John Henry Brown, or some damn thing—did not like me.

In 1947, someone was needed to help in the Rose Bowl Parade. For helping with the parade—I forget what I did: ride on one of the floats, or walk alongside—I was given a ticket to the Rose Bowl game, which was Michigan and Southern Cal.

After the parade, I went to the game, and in doing so, I missed a rehearsal. I was a stage manager and I was called on the carpet and read the riot act. You had to have discipline, and you just didn't miss rehearsals, and blah, blah, blah.

The powers that be made a big issue out of this. It was about two weeks before graduation and they kicked me out of the Playhouse. The only practical experience I'd had at the Playhouse was doing that play with George Reeves.

I moved from Pasadena to Hollywood. This was a period which is a complete blur in my memory. I was staying at the YMCA in Hollywood, on Wilcox, and I think living on my 52-20 club money, which was a G.I. Education Bill (if you were going to school, you got $20 a week for fifty-two weeks). It had been extended for six months. I still had very little money. I was paying something like $14 a week at the Y . . . and I was trying to write.

I was born in 1922, and someone had given me a 1922 silver dollar—it was my lucky charm. When *Red River* was playing on Hollywood Boulevard (I think it was the Vogue Theater), I went to a matinee. It cost ninety cents, so I plunked down my lucky silver dollar and went in to see one of the best westerns ever made.

Two hours later, I walked out of the theater, and I had one dime between me and the town. I think I ate peanuts that week, and finally there was an audition at Warner Bros. for an Errol Flynn picture—they needed fencers. And I could fence—I had learned in the army: the First Cavalry Division, Fort Riley, Kansas.

So I went over on this call to Warners. The movie was *Adventures of Don Juan* and they were hiring about twenty young guys who were fencers. They were in this fencing school, and Flynn was the teacher. Years later, I saw the picture, and it was one of these things where the students helped Flynn kill all the bad guys in a big action scene. It would have been a wonderful part, but they turned me down.

I decided then I was going to write for radio. I had some connections with somebody who knew of a comedy-western that was on Mutual Broadcasting called *Hash Knife Hartley*. It was based on a series of novels. They took the characters and did them in this radio show. I started writing for the show. The producers liked my work. They did about five or six of them. I now was getting paid—not much, but I was getting paid.

It was at that time I decided I didn't know how to write. There was a writing school down on Hollywood Boulevard—I forget its name, but they had some pretty good guest writers and lecturers, so I went. I had to attend twenty hours a week in order to be eligible for this G.I. Bill money.

I had gotten a job writing a daily fifteen-minute talk-radio show called *The Used Story Lot*. I was getting less to write the scripts than the typist was getting to type them up, but it was money. I was doing a daily fifteen-minute show on radio called *The Used Story Lot*, an hour show on Sundays, and *Hash Knife Hartley*. I was going to school twenty hours a week, to learn how to do what I was doing. That went on for almost a year.

    ✿   ✿   ✿   ✿   ✿

Then another fencing job came up over at Metro-Goldwyn-Mayer. It was *The Three Musketeers*. So I went over, and at that time Edward Arnold was the president of the Screen Actors Guild. I had known him in vaudeville when I was a little kid. He had done an act with Viola Dana. He didn't know me, but I remembered his act. So I went, and I got the part in this picture as a fencer, but I wasn't a member of the Actors Guild. I thought, Well, that's no problem—I'll just call Ed.

I called him, and he said, "I don't know what to tell you. You've never acted. You can't work unless you're in the Guild, you can't get in the Guild unless you work." The old catch-22, before the term even existed.

Billy Grady was the casting director at Metro. I thought, I'll just play along, and make the deal, sign the deal, and *then* I'll tell them I'm not a member of the Guild. I did, and they were very upset, but they worked it out, and I went to work on *The Three Musketeers,* fencing with Van Heflin and Gene Kelly; the director was George Sidney. It was marvelous. I fenced with everybody in a sequence that took about a week. I made a lot of money. And I remember the first check I ever got. Written in the background of the check in big, black letters was STUNT. So I got a stuntman's pay for the first four or five checks I got.

I was rich! I must have made a couple of thousand dollars. Now I was in pretty good shape. It wasn't costing me anything to live in Hollywood, and I got a chance to do a script for Harry Sherman's daughter. Harry was the producer of the *Hopalong Cassidy* films. I worked in a studio across from Paramount. I didn't have the foggiest idea what I was doing, but I wrote this script. It was a cavalry script called *Action Front*. When I finished, nobody paid any attention to it, but all along, I was learning the ropes of Hollywood.

After *Action Front*, the head of the wardrobe department at Universal, Manny Spack, had bought the rights to an O. Henry story in *Liberty* magazine called *The Adventures of Juan and Diablo*. He hired me to do a script for a television show. There wasn't much television at all then, but the idea was that it was going to be an hour TV show.

I did this script and gave it to Manny and he liked it very much. He was negotiating to do it as a series. I was hired to do five more. I think I was getting $400 a script, which was a fortune for me in those days. Then I did four more, and they liked them so much, they hired me for the rest. They were doing a total of thirteen, and I ended up doing them all.

Somewhere along the line, actor Paul Fix, over at Wayne Fellows (John Wayne and Bob Fellows had a company), read them, and thought they were really good. He talked Duke into having me come over to talk about buying these thirteen scripts. I was amazed that I was going to be talking to John Wayne, but I went in and I told Duke that I didn't own them. Manny Spack over at Universal did.

Manny Spack had made a lot of money over the years. There had been some merger coming up between Decca and MCA, buying Universal. Manny bought something like a hundred thousand dollars' worth of Decca stock, with the idea that it would be taken over by MCA, which it was. Manny became very wealthy.

Manny came in to talk to John Wayne about selling the thirteen scripts for *Juan and Diablo*. They had put under contract a young

Mexican kid named Gonzales Gonzales who had been in a number of pictures. He was in a Budd Boetticher picture over at Universal called *Wings of the Hawk*, and then he came over and worked in *The High and the Mighty*. He had a cute little part, as the ship's radio operator who stays in his chair and slides from one radio to the other while the ship tosses in the storm, so they put him under contract. Duke was always putting people under contract, like Anita Ekberg and Jim Arness.

As I mentioned, Manny was rich now. He went in to talk to Duke, who wanted to buy these thirteen shows. Duke's idea was for us to do the pilot for *Juan and Diablo* in Mexico. He was getting ready to do *Hondo* down in Camargo, Mexico, and would do the pilot of *Juan and Diablo* with the same crew down in Mexico. He was planning to use little Gonzales Gonzales.

So Duke offered Manny a deal. Manny, who had never been offered any kind of a deal on the project—nobody had ever read the scripts except the Wayne people—thought, I might as well hold out for money—he's certainly got it. Manny said no, he wouldn't sell it to him. And it never sold—I mean, to this day, nobody has ever seen it.

Duke said to me, "Well, why don't you stay here and write one just like it for Gonzales." Which I did, and it wasn't very good. It was a rip-off of *Juan and Diablo*, but it didn't work.

When I finished that, they said, "Well, why don't you write a screenplay for Duke." I had this title that I had used on a story years before, and had never made it or sold it: *Seven Men from Now*.

I took the title, they gave me an office and a legal pad and pencils, and I sat down in this little office at Wayne Fellows and wrote *Seven Men from Now*. After six weeks, I wasn't finished. They were paying me $250 a week for six weeks. I needed two more weeks to finish, and they said, "Okay, you can have the two weeks, but we're not gonna pay you. You can use the office and the pencils and the paper. You have to finish it, because it's no good to us the way it is."

I spent two weeks without pay, and I finished. The total cost to them was $1,500. Wayne didn't read it but I think Nate Edwards, the production manager, did. He said, "It's all right. There's a typical shoot-out in the rocks."

So nobody paid any attention to it, and it was there in a storage closet in the coffee room for about a year, along with about thirty or forty other scripts. They had me working on various things. I did a rewrite on a picture called *Gun the Man Down*, which was the first picture Andy McLaglen directed. Then they loaned me out to Fox, where I did a script. When I came back to work for Duke, somebody told me that they were looking for a picture for Bob Mitchum.

I took *Seven Men* to his producer—I forget his name—but he read it and liked it, and offered me $15,000 for the script. I went in to Duke and said, "These people must be crazy, 'cause you paid me fifteen hundred, but they want to give me fifteen *thousand*. I told them it's not my script. It belongs to Duke. I'll ask him and he'll probably want to sell it to you."

Duke said, "Now wait a minute, wait a minute. Let me read that." All of a sudden there was interest in *Seven Men from Now*. They had a ten-picture deal at Warner Bros. and had two more pictures to go. The two scripts they had at the office were a Ben Hecht script called *Quality of Mercy*, which they had paid $125,000 for, and my script for *Seven Men from Now*, which they'd paid $1,500 for. They wrote in big red letters, I remember distinctly, FIRST DRAFT. They sent *Seven Men* over, reluctantly, with *Quality of Mercy*.

Jack Warner read *Seven Men* and loved it, and said he wanted Duke to do it. But Duke was right in the middle of doing *The Searchers* at the time. He said, "Well, if they want to do it, let's get somebody to do it." They gave it to Joel McCrea, who didn't want to do it. They gave it to Robert Preston, and I don't think Bob ever read it, because he didn't like Hollywood too much at the time. Then they gave it to Randy Scott, who in turn hired Budd Boetticher to direct. *Seven Men from Now* was my first picture and was very well received. I went on to get Duke to buy an Elmore Leonard short story called "The Captives," which he paid $5,000 for and for which I did the screenplay.

When Wayne and Fellows broke up the company, as part of the deal, Fellows got *Quality of Mercy* and the Elmore Leonard story that I wrote the script for. He made a deal with Columbia for Randy Scott to do *The Tall T* (as this Elmore Leonard story was now called), with Budd Boetticher directing. Columbia made a deal—I think they paid him $17,000 for the script, with the proviso that I do any rewrite, and if I didn't do the rewrite, they wouldn't do the script.

Fellows came to me. We were not friends—he had done me dirt there a number of times, and was kind of a devious fellow. He had no talent at all except that his family had money. He said to me, "They want you to do this rewrite, and I'll give you a thousand dollars."

I said, "No. If I do a rewrite, I want a thousand dollars a page."

He said, "You've got me over a barrel."

I retorted, "I don't want you *anywhere*, but I'm not doing anything on the script unless I'm paid a thousand bucks a page."

As it turned out, it wasn't much of a rewrite. It was five pages, and I got $5,000 from Bob. What goes around comes around. Anyhow, that picture was made, and was successful and was well received. Randy Scott, Harry Joe Brown, and Budd formed a company which I became a part of. They asked me to write two original screenplays.

I had no idea what to do. I was getting $15,000 a script. I sat down and wrote *Ride Lonesome*, then *Comanche Station*. They were made for very little money—I mean *really* little money—but they were well received, and have a cult following here and in Europe. They're good pictures. Randy was very good, and Budd did a great job.

I went on to Warner Bros., where I did *Yellowstone Kelly* and *Fort Dobbs*. I worked on another script that I liked a lot called *The Whip*. To this day it's never been made. I tried to buy it back from Warner Bros., and was told they don't own it; they haven't any record of me having worked on it. It was thirty-some years ago, but they said they don't own it. Even so, I really can't make it, because if I do, they'll come out of the woodwork and nail me. That's happened to me on occasion and it's cost me more than I got to write it in the first place, so I don't want to do that again.

Next, I started to direct, and I did a picture up in Canada, *The Canadians,* which was a disaster. After that, I went back to doing television. I did a show called *The Lawman.* I did four of those, then I did a *Virginian.* Then I did six of the early *Combats,* which was very good training. The shows were good—two or three episodes were very good.

Following the television shows, I did *Mail Order Bride* in 1963 at MGM, with Buddy Ebsen, Lois Nettleton, and Keir Dullea. And that was a moneymaking picture—a little picture, but a moneymaker. The second picture I did at Metro was *The Rounders,* with Glenn Ford and Henry Fonda, in 1965. It didn't make a heck of a lot of money, but it was a good picture. I had written it from Max Evans's novel of the same name.

From there, I directed *The Money Trap,* which was a black-and-white Panavision picture with Glenn Ford, Rita Hayworth, Joseph Cotten, and Ricardo Montalban, plus a whole bunch of other people. A pretty good script, and not a bad picture.

Subsequently, I did *The Return of the Seven,* which was the sequel to *The Magnificent Seven.* It was all right; we didn't have much of a budget or any big-name actors except Yul Brynner, but it was all right. I came back and did *Welcome to Hard Times,* from the E. L. Doctorow book, with Henry Fonda. It has something of a cult following—it's a dark, dreary kind of a thing. I did *The War Wagon* with John Wayne and Kirk Douglas, which was a big success, followed by *Support Your Local Sheriff* with Jim Garner, which was an even bigger one.

I did about ten pictures after that, and I would say that the only ones that were really good were *Support Your Local Gunfighter* and *The Train Robbers. Hannie Caulder* is a western I did after *Gunfighter,* which a lot of people hate and a lot of people love. We made it for a million dollars in forty days—and it was pretty good. It comes up on television every once in a while.

Then the western began to fade. The reason for this has been kicked around for years. But I feel it's like any other trend in the picture business. For example, audiences became tired of gangster pictures, and they faded away. Still, make no mistake—the first time a western makes a lot of money, they'll be back!

Anyway, the sun began to set on the western, and I turned to television. But more about that later. . . .

I've been fortunate to work with some of the giants in the motion picture industry: John Wayne, Henry Fonda, Kirk Douglas, Robert Mitchum, James Garner, Glenn Ford, John Huston, Rita Hayworth, Walter Brennan, Angie Dickinson . . . the list goes on and on.

What follows is a story about Hollywood, the western movie, and all the people who have touched my life during the past half century of making motion pictures. It's my hope that some of my movies have touched your life, dear reader, as well.

Roll 'em.

1

John Wayne

"If you don't get that faggot ring off that sonofabitch, I'm walkin'
off the picture right now!"

We were in Durango, Mexico, making *The War Wagon,* starring Kirk Douglas and John Wayne. It was the first shot and Kirk
was wearing a fancy ring over a black velvet glove, on the little
finger of his gun hand.

I knew better than to argue with Duke, inasmuch as I was
making my first big-budget western. So I went along with him
and said, "I'd better get it off him now."

I'd hardly gotten the words out of my mouth when: "Don't
stand there, do it!" roared Duke.

A moment later we were both crossing toward Kirk. Once
there, I said, "Don't you think the ring is a little much, Kirk?"

Kirk gave me that champion grin and answered, "No, I think
it's just fine." Then, holding the ring up to Duke: "What do you
think, Duke?"

Duke didn't even bat an eye. He said, "It's great, just great."

That wasn't the first time Duke put a director out on a limb and cut it off. It wouldn't be the last.

*   *   *   *   *

While filming in Durango, we were staying at the Mexico Courts. It had about twenty cabins, and at that time it was the best place in town—but it was still pretty crummy.

Unfortunately, Duke's cabin was right next to mine. I was sharing this two-unit cabin with character actor Gene Evans. Gene was famous from Sam Fuller's *Steel Helmet* and lots of other movies.

On this particular day (which by the way was "Cinco de Mayo," the Mexican Independence Day), there was a big parade in the streets of Durango. Duke had decided to take a nap; he wasn't feeling well.

It must have been a Sunday. Gene Evans had been out shopping and he had bought an old, double-barrel, 12-gauge shotgun. It was so old that the wooden stock had rotted off. It had not been fired in at least a hundred years.

Gene was showing me this antique, and at the same time the Mexicans were celebrating Cinco de Mayo by shooting off firecrackers. It woke Duke up. He came crashing out of his cabin, still hearing explosions. The first thing he saw was me standing there holding the double-barrel shotgun. He yelled, "Here I'm trying to get some sleep, and you're shootin' that goddamn shotgun!"

"Duke, it hasn't been fired in a hundred years!" I yelled back at him.

"Bullshit!" He got in his car and stormed off down through the courts.

For many years after that, he'd see me and he'd say, "You're the guy who shoots shotguns while I'm tryin' to sleep!" What I should have done is shot Gene Evans.

*   *   *   *   *

The Duke was making a picture with Henry Hathaway called *The Sons of Katie Elder*, again in Durango. It was about two months after his lung operation and here he was at five thousand feet, doing a fight scene in an ice-cold river with two bad guys.

During the scene, his hat came off, and then his toupee. He was fighting for breath as he came out of the water when a photographer stuck a camera in his face and took a picture. Duke exploded.

"Get that sonofabitch outta here! Put him in a car and take him to the airport!"

A little later on that day, Duke and Henry were having lunch and Henry looked over and saw the cameraman being put into a car on his way to the airport. He said, "Duke, you were pretty rough on that guy. You know, he's from *Time* magazine, and we're gonna need all the help we can get when this picture comes out. What do you think?"

"Get him over here—lemme talk to him."

Someone got the guy out of the car and brought him over to Duke, and Duke said, "Look, you know, I had an operation about two months ago, and I was in that river and out of breath. It's five thousand feet and you stuck that goddamn camera in my face!" and he gave it to the guy all over again, gave it to him and threw him out again. That's the way Duke was.

On the other hand, Duke could be the most charming guy you ever met. He had a great sense of humor. And he had a trick he pulled on all of us. I caught on to it when he was getting older.

He had a way to make you think, when you'd run into him, that he had been thinking about you, or that you had some place in his life—which was a bunch of bull, because he never gave a rat's ass about you.

For instance, I was making a picture in Tucson once, and an award banquet was being given for Duke, David Dortort (the creator and producer of *Bonanza*), Michael Landon, and myself. I was working, so I couldn't go.

About two years later, Duke won the Academy Award for *True Grit*. I went to the awards ceremony down at the Music Center, or wherever it was. When it was over, I came out to get my car, and I spotted Duke.

He had the Oscar in his hand and all these cameramen and microphones in his face. As I walked by, he caught my eye, and I thought, Oops—I better say something to him. So I walked over, held out my hand, and said, "Congratulations."

Duke took my hand, pulled me up alongside of him, and said, "Where the hell were you in Tucson?"

In that way he made me think he *cared* whether or not I was in Tucson—which he didn't. He had a way of making you think he was thinking about you. It was a trick I'd seen him pull on many people, and we all fell for it.

✿   ✿   ✿   ✿   ✿

Then there was the time he bought season tickets to the Dodger games when Dodger Stadium was built. On opening day, Duke, his brother Bob Morrison, Duke's son Michael, and Tom Kane, their story man, were in the car together.

When they arrived at the stadium the traffic was slow-and-go, and Duke didn't have much patience. He kept seeing acres of empty parking spaces, but you had to keep going—traffic control officers filled them up from the top down or something. But reserved parking was included with the season passes, and Bob kept saying, "Duke, we have reserved parking."

And Duke said, "I don't give a damn! Let's park this goddamn thing!"

There were sawhorses set up to prevent parking in certain areas, so Duke ordered, "Stop the car!" He got out, threw a sawhorse aside, and yelled, "Park the car!" They parked it, and Duke commanded, "C'mon!" They started walking.

They walked into the stadium, but then nobody knew where their seats were. So Duke moaned, "Jesus, I paid twelve hundred dollars for seats, and you don't even know where they are?"

They finally found their seats, and they were down right behind the batter's box at ground level. In order to get there, it required walking down a ramp, and as you did, the whole stadium appeared before you. And as they walked down the ramp, sixty thousand people started to yell, "Duke! Duke!"

All of a sudden Duke forgot how mad he was, and he started

to think, *Boy, this is great!* They found their seats and sat down, and Duke was all smiles, with the crowd still chanting, "Duke! Duke!" But what he didn't realize was, the yelling was for Duke Snider, the Dodgers' star first baseman. And nobody ever dared tell him. To the day he died, I don't think he ever knew it . . . and I'm glad he's not going to be able to read it here.

* * * * *

Aside from the guys who took Duke's *Wild Goose* yacht into dry dock and cleaned the barnacles off it, I'm probably the only one who's ever seen it from the bottom.

I'd been with his captain on his shore boat, a Boston whaler, and we were at White's Landing over in Catalina. When we got back to the big boat and started to tie up, there was an outrigger and the captain was up front trying to tie up. Some waves came along and were about to shove the motors into the big boat. I immediately reached up to push 'em off.

At the same time the captain gunned the boat, it catapulted me over the motors, upside down. I hit my head right at the waterline of the *Wild Goose,* and went under. I was knocked out cold.

When I came to, my sunglasses were off. I could see them going down toward the bottom, and I thought, Well, if that's the bottom then I gotta go the other way. So I started swimming up, and I remember I could see Duke's kids swimming off the back of the boat, and I thought, Here I am drowning, and these kids are having fun.

I finally came up, and when I did, Duke reached over the side, grabbed me by the back of the neck, and pulled me up onto the boat. And he said, "I didn't think you were *ever* gonna come up!" He didn't go down to get me, even though he didn't think I was ever gonna come up.

I was filled with water—I'd almost drowned. And he was not shaken a bit. I sure was, but he wasn't. And that's what gave me the distinction of probably being the only guy who's ever seen the bottom of his wonderful *Wild Goose.*

* * * * *

There's a great Paul Fix story, one that Paul told me. Years ago, it would be in the 1930s, Paul was a writer—a good writer, as well as a good actor—and Paul and Duke were very good friends. Paul had written a play, and they put it on at a little theater, the Las Palmas in Hollywood. Duke was the stage manager and Paul was the star.

At one point during the show, Duke was to ring a bell for the phone. Paul was supposed to answer it. When Duke rang the phone, nothing happened. He rang it again.

Duke looked out to the stage and realized that he had forgotten to put the phone on the table upstage. So he grabbed a phone, ran backstage, and shoved his fist, with the phone in it, *through* the scenery. He dumped the phone on the table and pulled his hand back out, and as he did, Paul picked up the phone and said, "Hello?"

When the play was over Paul said, "What the hell did you do that for?"

Duke explained, "Well, I couldn't run out onstage with the damned thing—that was the only way to do it." And that was John Wayne, the stage manager.

Paul Fix tells another wonderful story. He and Duke were down in Camargo, Mexico, making *Hondo.* Wayne played the character of the same name, an Indian scout for the cavalry who always had a scroungy-looking dog with him. (The dog was actually kidnapped in Camargo and they were forced to pay a lot of money to get him back from the Mexican dognappers.)

There was a scene in *Hondo* where Duke comes into an Army tent. Paul was playing a colonel, but an actor was needed to play an orderly in the scene. This was a one-line part, I think. Usually, the director would just grab somebody to play these small parts, and this time it was Webb Overlander, who had been Duke's makeup man for many years. A little pain in the ass, but a good makeup man.

To pad his part, he decided to play his one line in German, and being a makeup man, he put on a German mustache—the kind that curls up on the ends, which looked ridiculous. In this scene, the gag was that Wayne walks down a Mexican street to the tent, pushes the flap of the tent aside, and comes in carrying a guidon, a troop flag. He has it in his hand, throws it on the colonel's desk, and says, "This is all that's left of C Troop." Paul looks at the flag and asks, "Those Indians you got this flag off of— were they dead Indians?" And Duke responds, "Finally." That's the scene.

As they were rehearsing, the director, John Farrow, had the camera in behind Paul and Webb Overlander, in the back of the tent, shooting out front. Duke came down the street with his dog, entered the tent, threw the flag down on the desk, and said, "That's all that's left of C Troop."

The director said, "Duke, could you put your weight on your right foot when you're standing there?" Duke said, "Okay." They rehearsed it again and when they got to the part where Duke says, "That's all that's left of C Troop," the director said, "Could you put a little more weight on your right leg?"

They repeated this four times, and finally Duke realized what the director was doing. When he came into the tent, the dog that was always with him sat down just inside the tent. The point was to get Duke to lean to his right so the dog would be in the shot. Well, that, number one, got Wayne mad, and he told Farrow, "You know what you should do here—the shot is very static. What you oughta do here is put your camera at the front of the tent, and as I come walking in, you pull back behind the desk here, and pull way back." As he said that, he felt the back flap of the tent. It was right up against a wall—of a church. So Duke said, "Why don't you give a director room to move around in? Who built this tent right up against the wall?" He began screaming for someone to get the art director and the set director out there right away.

Everyone waited and soon the art director, Al Yabarra, came in with the set director, and Duke said, "With all the room in this town, why did you put this tent right up against this wall? You don't give the director a chance to move around!"

They went on and on about this and concluded the church could not be moved—it had been there for six hundred years. Duke finally started to rehearse again. He turned and saw Webb

Overlander with his German mustache and said, "Who the hell are you?"

Webb replied, "I'm playing this part of the orderly as a German."

Duke said, "I don't care what the hell you're playing him as, take that goddamn mustache off!"

Attempting to explain, Webb pointed out that he had a whole background on this character he was playing—this character who had one line. He began, "You see, my background is that my father was in the Prussian Army, my folks were immigrants, and they moved out here to the frontier—"

Duke interrupted, "I don't give a good goddamn what your folks did! Get that thing off!"

Webb pulled the mustache off and the makeup crew had to be called in to cover up his upper lip where the glue had been and redo his makeup. This took about twenty minutes. Duke was sitting there thinking, waiting for them, and eventually he said to the director, "You know, this is too confining. This is not a good shot. Now, I'll tell you how to do this. Follow me."

Everyone left the tent, camera crew and all, and Duke pointed up a high hill. He said, "What you oughta do is put your camera up there and take a shot of me walking down the street. As I go into the tent, *then* you can cut to this shot." The director agreed.

The crew got the camera, the lights, and all the equipment and trudged to the top of this hill. Duke went up there, too, overseeing everything, and finally said, "Where's an assistant director?" He picked up the bullhorn and yelled, "Is there an assistant director on this picture?"

A guy slowly climbed up the hill, and when he got to Wayne he said, "It's time for lunch, Duke."

"Lunch? We haven't got a shot yet! We can't finish this picture if we're gonna waste all this time." After lunch, they finally got the three lines done . . . and Webb Overlander did not play his part as a German.

The director, John Farrow, had done many big hit pictures. And *Hondo* turned out to be another one.

I was about to do *The Train Robbers* with Wayne in Mexico and we went down to pick out the location. We had to build a train depot, some tracks, a barn, a water tower, a hotel, and a cantina. The art director went along with us as we laid it out the way we wanted to do it back at the studio.

The art director wanted to show Duke what we were up to, so he got a sheet of paper about three by four feet. On it he drew a square for the depot, a couple of lines to show the railroad tracks, a circle for the water tower, and then another square for the corral, one for the barn, one for the hotel, and one for the cantina. We brought Duke in to get his blessing on how we were going to build the set.

To show there were mountains in the background the art director had also drawn in little bumps with a marker pen to indicate their location. Duke looked at this sheet of paper lying on the floor and said, "The mountains are too close to the set."

I disagreed. "No, Duke, they are just right."

Duke got up off the couch, walked around this piece of paper, and said, "Come over here behind the barn and look. They're too close." And the barn was just a square drawn on a piece of paper.

We managed to assure him the mountains were fine and when the picture started, Duke walked onto the set and commented, "It's perfect." But back in the office they weren't perfect, especially behind the barn.

✿   ✿   ✿   ✿   ✿

Duke did have great instincts about the picture business, though. He knew when a scene wasn't working and what to do with it. He learned a great deal from John Ford. With all the films they made together, he learned by osmosis. It was uncanny how he could put a finger on something, although sometimes he was wrong. However, he was always wrong in the way he *presented* his argument. But he was a Woodrow Wilson man—if you didn't agree with him, you were wrong. Still, he was always trying to help, and once you realized that, you could learn a lot.

Of course, Duke had his chance to do everything his way when he made *The Alamo* and *The Green Berets*.

I directed two pictures with Duke. I was with him for seven years as a writer. Most everything I'd write for him, somebody else would make. There were two Randy Scott pictures that Budd Boetticher directed, which were good pictures. But because I was homegrown, Duke never really felt I could do anything. Later, I directed him in *The War Wagon,* which was a big success, and then *The Train Robbers,* which was a "little success."

He never got easier to direct. He was always tough. I remember, after *The War Wagon,* he went to make *The Green Berets.* People asked me, "Are you going to direct *The Green Berets?*"

And I said, "I'd rather *join* the Green Berets!"

❖   ❖   ❖   ❖   ❖

The last time I saw him was in the hospital, at UCLA, when he was dying of cancer. He was down to about a hundred pounds, and just looked awful. I went in to see him, and he put on the bold front. Duke always had a great sense of humor, right to the end.

I'd gone to see him in the morning with Al Murphy, an old friend of Duke's who'd worked for his company for years and years as a second assistant director. His name was really Al Silverstein, but Duke said, "I can't have an Al Silverstein workin' for my company. From now on, your name is Al Murphy."

Al and I were out in the hall, waiting, and a lot of dignitaries were visiting him. I remember Richard Nixon went in, as did a whole group of well-known celebrities. Eventually, his son Michael came out and said, "Duke will see you."

I said, "Look, just tell him we're out here. We don't have to go in and see him. I know he's tired."

And he said, "No, he wants to see you."

So we went in, and Michael came in with us and joked, "The reason Duke didn't want to see you was because Al Murphy is a Jew."

And Duke smiled and pointed up at the ceiling, and he said, "It's the *other* Jew I don't want to see." Yeah, he had a great sense of humor.

2

John Ford

Hawaii—1948
John Ford had bought a new shore boat, one of those mahogany Chris-Crafts with the red leather upholstered seats. It was a beauty. He and Duke had been ashore and were going back to the big boat. Duke was driving. He was also smoking a cigar and flicking his ashes out the side of the boat as they went.

When they got to the big boat and pulled up alongside, the whole backseat was on fire from the ashes on Duke's cigar! It burned out the whole backseat. But Ford didn't say a word. Even after they climbed aboard, he still didn't say anything.

Thirty years later, Duke had bought a house in Encino, complete with a projection room. And for this projection room, he'd bought some big, oversized furniture, special-made. One night, Ford and Duke were watching a movie, and Ford was smoking a cigar, his ashtray alongside of him on this brand-new couch.

When the picture was over the lights came up, and Ford, who had been flicking his cigar ashes in the ashtray, had burned a huge hole in the middle of this brand-new sofa. And he looked at Duke, and he said, "We're even." And Duke later said, "I knew *immediately* what he meant."

*　*　*　*　*

Most all the actors I worked with in the picture business somehow, at some time or another, were connected with or had worked with John Ford. For instance, Henry Fonda.

Henry was doing *Mr. Roberts,* and when Ford started the picture they were in Midway, I think, working on the boat. The first scene Hank did was with William Powell, who played the doctor. It's a long scene where Hank is telling Powell how he hates being on this cargo ship, and how he wants to be on a combat destroyer. It's a wonderful scene, and it goes on for about three minutes.

Ford rehearsed it a couple of times, and then he shot it. When he finished he said, "Now we're gonna do the fight scene with the crew." Hank was really upset because he had done the show on Broadway for many years, and he considered this scene with the doctor vitally important. He felt that Ford had sloughed it off.

So Hank was mad the whole day, and that night he went to Wingate Smith, who was Ford's first assistant, and told him he wanted to talk to the old man about what he thought had happened.

Ford was quartered in a old Navy barracks. He was sitting in an overstuffed chair drinking a beer, with an old-fashioned reading lamp over the top of the chair. Hank knocked at the door and went inside. Fonda relates, "I started to tell him what I thought, how I'd been in the play for all those years, and that this was such an important scene that we had done, and that I felt that he had not taken enough time. I got about a minute into my speech, and John Ford came out of his chair and hit me right in the jaw and knocked me down, jumped on top of me, and started hitting me in the face.

"Here I am, his leading man, the first day of the movie—and he's beating the hell out of me."

The lamp fell over on top of the two of them, and Wingate and some others came running in and pulled Ford off Hank and got Hank out of there. And Hank said that the next day, every time Ford would do a scene, he'd turn to Henry and say, "Was that good enough? Did that meet with your approval?"

Actually, they ended up being very bad friends on that picture, so much so, I don't think they ever worked together again. And they had done about seven pictures with each other before that, like *Young Mr. Lincoln,* and *The Fugitive* and *Fort Apache,* and of course the wonderful *Grapes of Wrath.* But from then on Ford was furious at Hank, and Hank was mad at Ford, because he was the one who got Ford on the picture.

✿　✿　✿　✿　✿

My favorite story about Hank Fonda is that he was doing a picture up in Jackson Hole, Wyoming—it was a timber picture called *Spencer's Mountain*—with Maureen O'Hara.

At one point in the film, Henry's father, played by veteran character actor Donald Crisp, is killed—a tree falls on him. It's very sad. So they're having the funeral, and the scene is that Henry is kneeling down at his father's grave and he reads this long, long monologue about how much he misses him, and how he never got a chance to tell him how much he loved him, etc. . . .

The director, Delmer Daves, who was a wonderful director but a highly emotional guy, had dug a hole at the head of this fake grave, behind the cross, and had the camera down in there, shooting up at Hank. Delmer was alongside the camera.

Hank did the scene; at the end of the scene he looked down and tears were streaming down Delmer Daves's face. And he looked up at Hank and he said, "Hank, that was terrible. Do it again."

Not many people know it, but Henry Fonda was a fine artist. Watercolors mostly—he did some oil, but watercolors mostly.

We did a picture together in 1966 called *The Rounders,* with Glenn Ford. We had a pickup truck that they used to carry the horse around in. And Hank did a painting—a watercolor—of that truck. It must have taken him two months, because the sun had to be exactly in the right position for him to paint. As a matter of fact, when the picture was over, he returned to Metro on the back lot, took the truck, and finished the painting—it took him about three more weeks. I still have the painting. It's one of my treasures.

Henry was a multitalented gentleman, a gentleman in every sense of the word. And one of the best actors that ever worked in Hollywood.

John Ford was making a picture up in Monument Valley and Paul Fix, an old friend of Duke's, thought he was going to get a job in it because he usually worked in Ford pictures. But on this particular picture, Ford did not hire him.

So Paul was griping about it to some actors and they mentioned it to Ford.

Ford got ahold of Paul Fix's agent and said, "Tell Paul to go over to Western Costume and have a costumer put an Indian outfit on him. Then send him on up to Monument Valley."

It was about a hundred and seventeen in the Valley—this was in July. So Paul went over to Western Costume and they put a buckskin outfit on him, and a big buffalo coat. This had all been arranged by Ford. They put a top hat on him, with a feather in it, and sent him off to Monument Valley.

Paul got in his outfit this one morning and went out to report to Ford. And he told Wingate Smith, the first assistant, "Tell Mr. Ford I'm here."

Ford walked over and there was Paul, standing in this buckskin outfit with a buffalo coat on and his top hat with a feather in it, and it's sweltering. Ford came up and looked at Paul and walked around him in a circle, and said, "The feather is too much. Take the feather out of the hat." So Paul took the feather out. And then Ford said, "And you can lose the fur coat." So Paul gladly took off the fur coat. And then Ford looked at him, and Paul had a bunch of beads on him, bear claws and that kind of stuff. So Ford said, "Lose the bear claws and all the beads and all that crap." So Paul did. Ford looked at him for a long time, and he finally said, "No, it's not gonna work. Forget it. Go home."

Joel McCrea tells the story that Ford was doing a picture, *The Iron Horse*. They had laid a bunch of track up in Monument

Valley, because they were building this railroad in the picture. They had all these Chinese workers laying the track—hundreds of them. And they had hundreds of Indians.

On this particular day, the actors all got dressed and came out, and they started to work. They were working on the train, doing a scene, and it started to snow. So Ford said, "Well, that's a wrap. We can't work—it's snowing."

So the actors went back (they were living in tents) and took off their makeup, took off their outfits, and started to play poker, about six or eight of them.

Well, Ford looked over, and he saw all these guys having a good time playing poker, so he called Wingate Smith, and he said, "Listen. I want you to get the extras ready. But I want the Chinese dressed in the Indian outfits and I want the Indians dressed in Chinese outfits."

Wingate was smart enough not to ask him why, and he just said, "Yes, sir," and took off.

Ford waited about an hour while all the extras got dressed. Then he went over to the poker game, and he said, "C'mon, guys—I've decided to work."

It had stopped snowing, but there was snow all over. So they broke up the poker game, and he got the guys back in their outfits, and got them in makeup, and around two in the afternoon they dragged out to the set. They got up on the train to finish the scenes that they were doing, and Ford looked out at the extras. Here were these Chinese dressed like Indians, with queues hanging down the backs of their heads, and Indians dressed in these Chinese outfits with mandarin collars and little slippers. Ford said to Wingate, "Wingate! The Chinamen are dressed like Indians and the Indians are dressed like Chinamen!"

Wingate knew better than to say, "You told me to do it," so he said nothing.

Ford yelled, "Well, for God's sake! I can't work—forget it."

So after getting the actors to break up their poker game, and to get back in costume and makeup, he called it off. He was famous for doing stuff like that.

On the 1948 movie *Three Godfathers* there was a scene where these three outlaws had robbed a bank, and when they get out in the desert they find a wagon with a woman in it who's going to have a baby. She finally has the baby and dies. And these three bandits have to get the baby back to civilization—in effect, turn themselves in.

So they're struggling across the desert with this baby. And in this one scene, they were going up a hill and Ford said, "Now the three of you go up that hill." Then he got Harry Carey Jr. aside who was nicknamed "Dobie," and he said, "Now, you see that rock up at the top of the hill? Go to the left of that rock." And Dobie said, "Okay." And Ford said, "Action," and up they went.

Dobie went to the left of the rock, and Ford yelled, "Cut! I said to the right of the rock! Now come back—we gotta do it again."

Not only did they have to do it again, they had to get all the tracks out of the sand so that it didn't look like take two . . . and it took them about a half hour, and there they went again. And just before they were going, Ford went over to Dobie and he said, "No matter what I say—go to the left of the rock."

Well, about the fourth time he did this, Duke and Pedro Armendariz were furious with Dobie because they thought he was doing it on his own, and they were about to kill him. Finally, Ford let him do it right. Dobie has written a book called *Company of Heroes* that details all his adventures with Ford, and it's really good reading. Ford was a cantankerous old guy, but he was a hell of a director.

I guess the most famous story about Ford was in the silent days when he was making westerns over at Universal. They brought the financial big shots of Universal out from New York to watch Ford work.

When the director came on the set, this one big shot said to him, "Do something exciting."

So Ford got the cowboys, a whole bunch of them, to ride down the middle of this street, firing their guns. And everybody thought it was wonderful.

Then this big shot said, "Now do something else that's exciting." So Ford set fire to the sets. The street burned down.

And the people thought it was wonderful.

        ❀   ❀   ❀   ❀   ❀

Robert Parrish, who was a film editor and cutter, and later a director, cut a couple of documentaries for Ford during World War II. One was *Midway,* and the other one was called *December 7th.* Later Parrish got an Oscar for editing *Body and Soul,* a famous fight picture. Then he went on to direct some very good pictures.

He tells a story about when Ford was making *How Green Was My Valley.* Parrish was cutting a picture, I think at Fox. Ford sent word to Bob to come out on the set, and one morning he went out and Ford was standing in the middle of the set with a finder up to his eyes, and just looking around.

Without lowering the finder, Ford said, "Bob, I hear you wanna be a director. Come over here."

So Bob went over and stood alongside of him and Ford, without taking his eyes out of the finder, said, "Now this is your first lesson in becoming a director. Some mornings you come to work, and you won't have the foggiest idea what to do. And when that happens, you take the finder off the camera, and you stand out in the middle of the set, and you put it up to your face and look around. It's better if you close your eyes, because then you can concentrate better. And in about ten minutes, some production guy will call the front office and say, 'The director hasn't got a shot yet.' Then about fifteen minutes after that, some creep— some associate producer—will come .out on the set, and he'll come up alongside of you and ask some silly question like, 'Anything wrong?' When he does that, you swing around like this. . . ."

Bob said that at this point Ford swung this finder around and hit him right on the head, drawing blood. Ford then continued, "You can get so good at it, you can get two or three associate producers a week. That's your first lesson in directing, and it's very important. Now go back to you cutting room." And that was Bob Parrish's first lesson as a director.

❀   ❀   ❀   ❀   ❀

In later years, when he was doing *Cheyenne Autumn*, Ford had become addicted to pills, and he was drinking, and he'd take these uppers, and it was really wiping him out, so that he could hardly get up in the morning.

Bill Clothier, the famous cameraman, had the assignment of getting him out of bed in the morning and getting him onto the set. One particular morning, Bill woke him up and went into the bathroom, and there were all these pills in the medicine cabinet that Ford had been taking. So Bill threw them down the toilet and flushed it. Then he went out to wait in the car for Ford to get dressed.

In about fifteen minutes, Ford came storming out to the car, got in, and said, "Some sonofabitch flushed my pills down the toilet."

Clothier replied, "I did."

Ford roared, "What would you do if I flushed all your *lenses* down the toilet?"

❀   ❀   ❀   ❀   ❀

For quite some time, I have wanted to do a stage play about John Ford's last days, titled *If I Should Die Before the Wake*. The entire play would be set in Ford's bedroom, with all the dialogue and action revolving around Ford in his bed. In fact, John Ford, in his own way of giving up, refused to get out of bed for many months. He would entertain visitors quite frequently. Always beside his bed were a pair of tennis shoes, which he would point to as soon as a guest arrived and explain, "I have just been out jogging and overworked myself." He would then reach into his plastic bucket for a cigar.

Bob Parrish went to see Ford shortly before the great director died of cancer. He was greeted at the door by a nurse who informed him the doctor had limited visitors to one a day, and for only five minutes—no exceptions. Ford was thin, but still wearing the familiar patch over his eye, sitting up in bed with a cigar. He asked about Bob's wife and mother and when he saw Bob looking at his watch, he said, "What are you looking at your watch for?"

"The nurse told me I could only have five minutes."

"How the hell come? [Director George] Stevens only got five minutes, [director Frank] Capra got five, and [director Howard] Hawks got five. Tell you what, you came a long way. There was another director came to see me yesterday. He was a dull sonofabitch. I threw him out after two minutes. You can have his other three."

They talked for over an hour. Ford asked Bob if he had won any more Oscars and Bob shook his head no. Ford looked him straight in the eye and said, "It turns out they're not as unimportant as I thought—win as many as you can. Take care of yourself, Bob. You're a good lad."

Ford was scrounging in his plastic bucket for another cigar when Bob left.

3

John Huston

John Huston: a great director, and a royal pain in the ass. He wrote and directed one of my favorite movies of all time, *The Treasure of Sierra Madre*, for which he was awarded Academy Awards for both writing and directing.

He worked as an actor in two of my movies. The first one was a picture that was released under the title of *The Deserter*, and Huston was to play a tough, old general. I went to Rome, and the script wasn't really great, so I did a rewrite. When I finished it, I decided to go to Ireland. I think it was something to do about a horse for my daughter—a jumping horse.

So I took my daughter, and my then-wife, and I took a copy of the new script with me. I had Huston's phone number; I figured to call and get his address and send the script to him. He was in Loughrea, just outside Galway, Ireland.

When I landed in Dublin I checked into the great old Gresham Hotel and called Huston. It was about seven o'clock in the evening, and I introduced myself and told him I had a new copy of the script, and I didn't trust sending it by the mail from Rome to Dublin. I told him I was in Ireland, and I said I was going to mail the script, and I wanted his address. He said, "No, you're not going to mail it. You're going to bring it over here." It was a Paramount Picture, and he said, "Go to the Paramount office there in Dublin, get a car and driver, and come on over here." He insisted on it.

I said, "I have three people with me."

And he said, "That's all right, I have a castle. I have rooms all over the place."

I hung up and said to my wife, "What a wonderful guy. Warm, charming . . ."

So, the next morning I got ahold of the Paramount people, got a car and driver, loaded everybody in, and had us go clear across Ireland to Loughrea. We pulled up in front of this Georgian mansion, and I got out of the car and went to the front door, and Huston opened the door. And he said, "Yes?"

I said, "I'm Burt Kennedy. I'm bringing over the script for this picture we're going to do."

He said, "Oh, wonderful, wonderful." He took the script and said, "Where are you staying?"

I said, "In Galway."

"What hotel?"

I said, "The big one."

At that point, his assistant, Gladys Hill, realized what had happened. She said, "Oh, no, no, no—you're going to stay here."

I said, "Well, I have three people with me."

She said, "No, that's no problem."

So we got out of the car, and I was really embarrassed, because John Huston had been drunk when I talked to him, and he didn't remember talking to me at all.

We went into this beautiful home. Huston was about half-friendly. We stayed for the evening meal. There were about twenty people there, but Huston never introduced anybody. He dressed for dinner; he was the country gentleman. He sat at the head of the table and held forth all during the meal. As I say, he was a royal pain in the ass—with emphasis on the "royal."

Anyway, I was so upset that the next morning I was up at five o'clock. I said, "Let's get the hell out of here." I said good-bye to John and Gladys Hill and went on back to Dublin, very embarrassed by the whole thing. We went on to make the picture, and only had one or two fights. On the whole he was fine.

When I got back after that picture, I had breakfast with Duke over at his house in Encino, and I was telling him about how I didn't get along with John Huston. He said, "Neither did I," and went into a story about when they were making *The Barbarian and the Geisha.*

Wayne was playing Townsend, a U.S. statesman in Japan, and in this one scene he was on a horse in a parade. Huston's measure of a man was how well he could ride a horse. I've talked to many actors about this. John tried to get them thrown off and he put them on horses when he shouldn't have.

Duke recalled, "I'm on this big, white stallion, who's snortin'. . . ." In the parade, there were about two thousand extras. So Huston got a bunch of little Japanese kids, and he had them light firecrackers and throw them at the feet of Duke's horse. And Duke said, "I suddenly realized that the sonofabitch was trying to get me thrown off this horse in front of all these people." He wanted John Wayne to be thrown on his ass.

"I said to myself, *if* I get thrown, and *if* I can get up, I'm gonna kill him." Well, luckily for Huston, Duke was not thrown off the white horse, because knowing Wayne, he *would've* killed him.

4

Jack Elam

A man with a face only a mother and millions of western fans can love, Jack is a dear friend of mine. We have done fifteen films together. He is a world-class actor and poker player. Most players just hand over their money to him when they sit down to play poker . . . it saves time.

Jack started in the picture business as an accountant. He was also the night manager of the Beverly Hills Hotel, and a prime mover in the building of the famous Bel-Air Hotel.

Rawhide was his first big break in the picture business. He replaced an actor in Lone Pine, California, after the film started. To this day he will not name the actor he replaced for fear of hurting his feelings. On that film he became friends with Tyrone Power and he credits Power with helping him learn the ropes in the early days.

Jack looked lean and mean in those days, and he was cast as the bad guy for years. He was so identified with being a heavy that United Artists thought I was crazy when I wanted him for the comic deputy in *Support Your Local Sheriff*. I knew Jack was a riot personally and that he'd be great. He was, and it started a whole new career for him. We next did *Support Your Local Gunfighter*. Jack was so funny in that, I had a hard time casting him in a straight role from then on. I did a pilot called *Sidekicks* for CBS and when I ran it for the powers that be at the network, they were mad because they said Jack was too funny. They wanted me to cut some of his scenes. I refused.

A couple of months ago Jack and I were invited to a western film festival in Memphis. Jack spent three solid days signing autographs. There were five hundred people waiting in line to meet him. He is a special guy and a special friend.

I try to use Jack whenever possible, because he's what we in Hollywood call a "scene stealer." In addition to *Support Your Local Sheriff* and *Support Your Local Gunfighter,* I cast him in *Hannie Caulder* in 1971, where along with Ernest Borgnine and Strother Martin he played one of a trio of murderous brothers. Together they stole the movie right out from under Raquel Welch and Robert Culp.

As I mentioned, Jack was usually cast as a heavy in the early part of his career, which has spanned half a century. You may remember him in 1955's *Kiss Me Deadly* as one of Albert Dekker's henchmen, or as a deadly gunslinger in 1954's *Cattle Queen of Montana*, which starred Barbara Stanwyck and future president Ronald Reagan. That same year, he costarred with Gary Cooper, Burt Lancaster, and Ernest Borgnine in *Vera Cruz*. He was blown out of his saddle by Charles Bronson in 1964's *Four for Texas* and again four years later in *Once Upon a Time in the West*. He popped up—quite memorably—in *High Noon*, as the town drunk.

Jack's TV credits virtually span the history of the medium itself, starting in 1954 with *Gangbusters* and continuing right up to a recent appearance on Tim Allen's *Home Improvement*. He's guested on *Gunsmoke, Rawhide, Cheyenne, Have Gun Will Travel, Zane Grey Theater, The Rifleman, The Lawman, Daniel Boone, The Wild Wild West,* and dozens of other shows. He was a regular on *The Dakotas* in 1963 and in *Temple Houston* later that year; in *The Texas Wheelers* in 1974, opposite Gary Busey and a pre–*Star Wars* Mark Hamill; in *Detective in the House* in 1985, and in *Easy Street* in 1986.

"I started in the picture business after World War II, around 1946," Jack says. "As an accountant at the Sam Goldwyn Studio. I didn't start acting until '48 or '49. My first picture was something called *The Judge Has an Alibi*. The budget was twenty thousand dollars. It starred Lee Lassis White, who was a kind of western singing star in those days. An old grouchy singing star.

"My first real break was on a picture called *Rawhide* in 1951, with Tyrone Power and Susan Hayward, for Twentieth Century-Fox. At that time, I was working with John Barrymore Jr. on a picture called *High Lonesome*. Frank Nugent who wrote *The Searchers*, directed it. John Jr. was sixteen years old then and a nice kid, but a loose cannon. I had to live with him to keep him out of trouble.

"When I got back from location there was a message from my agent—I had to be in [Darryl F.] Zanuck's office at six A.M. They ran some film on me, a scene from a TV series called *The Changes of Eddie Drake*. I played the heavy. Zanuck said, 'He's the one.' They put me on Zanuck's private plane and sent me to Lone Pine and I did the move *Rawhide*, with Susan Hayward and Tyrone Power.

"I was put under contract to Fox for seven years. Which lasted one year. They didn't give me anything to do, so I begged out of it. I was friends with Tyrone Power; he was very nice to me. I was a young kid, and suddenly I was in the big time. Ty was great. Henry Hathaway was the director, and he was no bargain for a young kid like me.

"Well, they were so impressed with my work in *Rawhide* that Tyrone Power asked for me in his next picture, *An American Guerrilla in the Philippines*. I was over in the Philippines for three and a half months on that fucking thing—and I worked two days! But Ty wanted me over there. Fritz Lang directed it. I did *Rancho Notorious* for him in '52, with Marlene Dietrich and Arthur Kennedy. The same year I did a two-day on *High Noon*.

"I did *Vera Cruz* for Robert Aldrich in 1953. I had some problems with Burt Lancaster on that picture. He sort of had this superior attitude. And a gang of us, who played heavies—there was Ernie Borgnine and Charles Bronson (he was still Buchinski then); we were nothing at the time. One day, Lancaster had his kids on the set, and he called them over and he said, 'Hey, look at his eyes.' He was making fun of my eyes. I don't mind when my friends do it, but I think Burt was out of line there. We all know the story of my eyes—they don't line up. We had a fight on the set that Aldrich had to break up. Gary Cooper, who was the other star of that show, was a tremendous gentleman, and I got to know him quite well. He'd buy me a drink and say, 'Jack, don't let this sonofabitch get to you.' "

The late Henry Hathaway was a fine director, but he was a tough SOB—ask any actor who worked with him. William Wellman was another first-rate director, but also a tough guy. He made some excellent movies, most notable among them *The Ox-Bow Incident, Battleground,* and *The High and the Mighty.* For Wellman, Jack did *My Man and I* in 1952.

"One day on the set," Jack recalls, "I went to my dressing room to go to the bathroom, which was way across the lot. At the same time, I was needed on the set. By the time they got me, Wellman had been waiting for about five minutes. When I came in, he said, 'We've been waiting for you for over an hour. Don't you know you're supposed to be on the set?' And I said, 'I had to take a shit.' Wellman fell down—he thought that was the funniest thing he ever heard in his life. From then on, he made fun of me being ugly, though not in a nasty way. 'Goddang,' Wellman would say to me. 'How'd you get so ugly?' I'd say 'I don't know, I been sick. What's your excuse?' "

Jack did two movies with John Wayne: *The Comancheros* in 1964 and *Rio Lobo* in 1970. In 1972, I wanted to cast Jack in *The Train Robbers,* opposite Wayne and Ann-Margret. Wayne balked at this, because in *Rio Lobo,* Jack stole the picture away from him, or so the critics claimed.

"The reviewers came out and said, 'Wayne better keep Elam with him.' That aside, I got along very well with him. Duke said to me years ago, 'There's four reasons that I'm as successful as I am, and that's Howard Hawks, William Wellman, John Ford, and Henry Hathaway.'

"David Huddleston, the Duke, and I were playing liar's poker in Duke's dressing room one day during the shooting of *Lobo*. It was David who told the story about how there are five stages of an actor's life:

1. "*Who* is Jack Elam?
2. "*Get* me Jack Elam.
3. "Get me *a* Jack Elam.
4. "Get me a *young* Jack Elam.
5. "Who is Jack Elam?"

Jack did a nice piece of work for director Sam Peckinpah in the 1973 *Pat Garrett & Billy the Kid*. (He gets gunned down by Kris Kristofferson's Bill Bonney.) Peckinpah's drinking was legend around Hollywood. When William Holden died after hitting his head on a coffee table and bled to death in 1982, Peckinpah said, "It isn't the booze that gets us, it's the goddamned coffee tables. Get rid of the coffee tables." Sam once said to Lee Marvin, when they were drunk, "I hate all actors." To which Lee replied, "All actors do."

"We were in Durango [filming *Pat Garrett & Billy the Kid*]. I only worked three days, and Sam carried me for two and a half months. I made a hatful of money on that. The studio head came down twice and said, 'Finish Jack.' And Sam would say, 'I can't figure where to do the shot. I need to take him to the location.' The studio guy said, 'Take it [the scene] out of the picture.' He didn't."

I asked Jack what kind of picture he'd like to go out on. He responded with, "I'd like to do another big western comedy. As long as I don't have to ride a bicycle."

Sounds good to me.

5

My Diary

June 26, 1969
Arrived Rome to direct *The Deserter*. Called Karl Malden, Ernie Borgnine, Hank Fonda, Richard Boone, Marty Balsam, and Marty Landau. Western Costume: two hundred and twenty cavalry outfits. Boots, hats, belts, and twenty-five scouts. Lunch with Dino De Laurentiis at his studio.

June 28, 1969
Karl Malden wants $250,000; $1,500 a week expenses; two tickets to Rome. Call Richard Boone; Herb Solo at Metro.

July 2, 1969
Back at Los Angeles. Lunch at MGM with Herb Solo (worldwide head of MGM) and Paul Kohner (a top agent, handling mostly European actors and actresses). The cavalry outfits are $35.75 apiece; $60 per officer and $35.70 per scout. Sooner or later,

we're gonna have trouble with boots, and are probably going to have to make them over in Rome.

July 7, 1969
Talked to Frank Sinatra in New York, reference *Dirty Dingus Magee*. Meeting him in New York on my way to Rome.

July 8, 1969
TWA to New York. Checked into the Waldorf Tower. Talked to Frank Sinatra—will see him tomorrow.

July 9, 1969
TWA flight to Rome. Wire Frank Sinatra—remind him of *Murphy's War*, the book that he wants to do.

July 11, 1969
Flew to Split, Yugoslavia. Private jet. Locations no good. Back to Rome, Flight 406. Wire Dick Lyons, reference Sinatra.

July 15, 1969
Leaving for Spain. Talked to Herb Solo at MGM. Looks good for January start, Sinatra. Talked to Herb Tobias, my agent. Trying to get Ricardo Montalban and Patrick Wayne for roles in *The Deserter*.

July 16, 1969
Arrived Madrid. Waited four hours for plane to Almería. Arrived Almería at six o'clock. Found locations and the fort. Leaving for Málaga tomorrow. Have to find river crossing.

July 21, 1969
Trying to get Jack Elam and Bobby Walker Jr. Found locations. Have a script from Frank Sinatra. Bobby Walker said no. Elam said no—they're both working.

August 1, 1969
In Madrid, trying to set Brandon de Wilde and Pat Wayne. Got
'em.

August 6, 1969
Meeting with Dino De Laurentiis. Got back script for Frank
Wolf—an actor I wanted in the picture—but he killed himself
while he was working on another picture. Problem at MGM.
They're selling off the back lot and all the props. Heading for
Dublin.

August 14, 1969
Looks like MGM deal is in trouble because of takeover by Kri-
korian. Arrived in Dublin. Called Bob Mitchum; John Huston to
deliver script of *Backbone*.

August 17, 1969
Arrived John Huston's place. The big, bad, and beautiful. Huston
is a pompous pain in the ass—just right for the picture. He's
playing a general in *The Deserter*. Leaving today for Dublin and
the riots. Then to Rome Monday. Chuck Connors called—a
younger pain in the ass. Staying at John Huston's estate is like
dying and going to heaven by mistake. Returned to Dublin.

August 19, 1969
Huston conflict of start dates—trying to get Henry Fonda. Pepe
Lopez arrived from Spain—my first assistant.

August 20, 1969
Just received a wire from Robert Evans saying he insists on
Techniscope. First sign of a bad picture is when the company
insists you do things their way. Bottom of the bill, here we come.
    Things I've learned in Europe: If there are clouds over St. Pe-
ter's, it'll rain in Rome. If there's a mist over the Irish Sea, it'll
be clear in Dublin. If Dino De Laurentiis doesn't shake hands
when you come into his office, there's gonna be a big storm.

Talked to Bob Evans. He said stand firm on Huston and no one eight-five ratio (which is a form of wide screen, such as CinemaScope and Panavision).

August 22, 1969
Made a handshake deal with Dino De Laurentiis for a Rolls-Royce if I rewrite the script for nothing.

August 30, 1969
Rome. Two guys are here to sign me for a ten-million-dollar picture, and they ran out and left a bad check for the hotel. Clerk thinks I'm in business with them. Every time the manager sees me in the lobby, he yells, "What about that bad check?"

I signed the MGM deal. To rewrite, produce, and direct *Dirty Dingus Magee*.

Leaving for Madrid in the morning. Went to see Harry Jackson, who had the *Time* magazine cover of John Wayne in *True Grit*. He's clever. Made me pay for his book—damn clever.

September 1, 1969
Arrived in Madrid. Went out to see the horses. Saddles are a problem. Seems we have one hundred horses and they bought twenty-five saddles.

Staying in the same room at the Castellana Hilton where I stayed when I came here to make *Return of the Seven*. I hope that isn't a bad sign.

September 7, 1969
Left Madrid for Málaga location at Antequera. Drove from Málaga to Almería—six hours, twenty-three hundred curves. Turned down the set and found another.

Just discovered I'm only forty-seven. I thought I was forty-seven last year.

My agent called to tell me we got a bad review on *Young Billy Young*. Didn't surprise me inasmuch as it's a bad picture.

We start Thursday—I'm ready.

September 10, 1969
The Deserter starts tomorrow—I'm ready.

September 11, 1969
First day on the picture—no problems. Our cast is gonna be good. Rained-out half day. Dino wants to know how I'm gonna cut the script to make up the time. Here we go again—no one in this damn business worries about the right thing. Called everybody a no-good sonofabitch and went back to work.

September 14, 1969
Free day—Sunday—I feel like a fighter between rounds. Hotel manager just informed me that Chuck Connors wants his water supply purified twice. Glad it's Sunday—that'll give me all day to get it done.

   Had lunch with Ricardo Montalban—a wonderful actor and a wonderful man.

   My agent, Herb Tobias, sent me a good-luck wire on the first day of the picture. Trouble is, it's in Spanish. He probably got a rate.

September 17, 1969
Did big action sequences today. I told the Italian cameraman to be careful around the horses—his first western. Cameraman stepped on by a horse—now he's careful.

September 19, 1969
Wardrobe Chuck Connors, Ian Bannen, Brandon de Wilde, Albert Salmi, and Woody Strode. Had to let them go early to see El Cordobés fight a bull. Tomorrow they all work.

September 20, 1969
Haven't seen any dailies. Seems there's an Italian law says you have to have four thousand feet to ship it out of the country. There's another law says you save money if you do it that way. I hope I never have to make another picture over here.

October 2, 1969
Two dogs in the picture had a fight. One had to go to the hospital.

October 3, 1969
Two actors had a fight. One went to the hospital.

This is the worst crew I've ever worked with. The cameraman is trying to win an Academy Award. The picture is rotten so far, but I have a chance when we get to the scenes. Leaving for Málaga tomorrow.

October 4, 1969
Went to work in a driving rainstorm—road washed out. Cast spent six hours in car getting to location. Sun came out at three o'clock. My star Bekim Fehmin refused to work—he left for Málaga. Floodwaters cut us off from the hotel. Bekim went by boat; it capsized, and he swam ashore. We crossed the flood at eleven-thirty at night—damn near lost our car in the water.

October 16, 1969
The sun came out. A horse fell off a bridge. He lived—a miracle. The first one on this picture. I think we need another one—when it opens.

October 24, 1969
Finished mountain stuff. Rained fifteen days—leaving for Almería tomorrow.

November 23, 1969
Finished picture. Was a struggle—I think I won, but you never know.

Left for L.A., stopped in Paris and London—lost my god-damned bumper chute.

December 23, 1969
MGM can't make up their mind about Frank Sinatra starring in *Dirty Dingus Magee.*

January 2, 1970
George Kennedy signed to go into *Dingus* with Sinatra. Harry Stradling Jr. is gonna be the cameraman. Hollywood is on its ass. It's a shame, but it'll come back.

January 3, 1970
Leaving for locations in Arizona. Guess I have to make the damn thing.

January 20, 1970
John Lee Mahin, the writer, came for lunch at Metro—had to have a pass. He helped build Metro-Goldwyn-Mayer.

James Garner wants to make *Latigo* [which turned out to be *Support Your Local Gunfighter*]. I think I can make it in late summer. Everybody out of work—I feel guilty, but then again, I'm making jobs for people so I guess it all adds up.

February 3, 1970
Left for Arizona to film *Dirty Dingus Magee*. Jim Aubrey, the head of Metro, wants me to fire Anne Jackson and get another actress. Here we go again. I threatened to quit. They backed down. Hate to have to do it this way, but that's showbiz.

February 20, 1970
Bill Finnegan, a production manager, flew in today. I think I bought *The Insurrection*. It's a great book. Sinatra flies to Washington today—a show for a new congressman. I think Danny Thomas is on the set today—funny man.

February 23, 1970
Started Frank Sinatra today—he's very good. He flies to work in his helicopter at eight-thirty. Picked up two days on the schedule. Picked up another day. Frank works hard.

March 27, 1970
Finished *Dirty Dingus Magee*.

May 18, 1970

They're having a big auction at MGM, auctioning off all the wonderful properties. I suggested a new trademark—an auctioneer screwing a lion.

August 5, 1970

Flew to Durango, Colorado, to look at train for *Latigo*. Getting into Denver on the 7th. I previewed *Dirty Dingus Magee*. Reaction was very good. I start *Latigo* next Monday. I'm ready.

August/September 1970

Starting *Latigo* tonight. I want to call it *Hell Bent for Purgatory* but nobody else does, so we decided to call it *Support Your Local Gunfighter*.

September 10, 1970

Gunfighter is still going one day ahead—I think it's good. Just signed to do another picture at Warners, *Skin Game*.

September 18, 1970

Finished "*Gunfighter*." Might be a good picture. Had a fight with Jim Garner next-to-the-last night. He played movie star on me.

Talked to Norman Bare, the line producer; he said Dino is sending me another script. The hell you say.

September 23, 1970

Last week Pauline Kael in *The New Yorker* said I make "Freudian, freaky westerns."

December 2, 1970

Left for London via TWA. Going to make picture starring Raquel Welch [*Hannie Caulder*]. Raquel is playing woman gunfighter in a serape. Sergio would probably call it *A Titful of Dollars*.

December 3, 1970
I'm in London, and they've set me up in an office in Rogers and Cowan's. We're on the tenth floor and there's a sign on the door that says IN CASE OF FIRE, GO TO THE WINDOW AND JUMP TO THE ADJOINING ROOFTOP. Jesse Owens couldn't make it—it's forty goddamn feet!

December 7, 1970
Twenty-nine years ago the Japs bombed Pearl Harbor. This week I bombed London with *Dirty Dingus Magee.* Leaving for Madrid in the morning.

December 23, 1970
Ran into John Huston at the Hilton in Madrid. We got drunk and decided to make a steeplechase picture with my daughter's horse. Also made plans to partner in a picture in Africa. Great idea for a film. We both would probably end up in the elephant burial ground. Huston is still a pompous pain in the ass, but I like him.
    Leaving for London on the 22nd, back to Madrid on the 29th.

December 25, 1970
This is the second Christmas at the Hilton in Madrid that I've spent alone. Miss my kids, but they're fine.

December 26, 1970
What the hell happened to Christmas? Left Madrid for London.

January 2, 1971
New year—starting *Hannie Caulder* on the 18th. I'm ready.

January 9, 1971
David Haft is the producer of *Hannie Caulder*. He thinks he's a writer—what he says goes. I hope he doesn't say Raquel Welch, because without her, we have no film. Pat Curtis, Raquel's husband, says he's the boss, and what he says goes. Wish to hell he'd say David Haft.

January 1971

The company ran out of money and I'm now in Dublin, Ireland, where the girls are not pretty. If I ever saw a place needing a street-sweeper, this is it. I think they got the "wearin' o' the green" from the mold.

March 18, 1971

Sitting at a studio in London called Twickingham. Waiting for the film to come in. Time for decision—I either cut the picture or cut my throat. Like I've always said, success is getting up one more time than you get knocked down.

May 31, 1971

It's hard to believe, but I'm on a plane to New York, then out to see a cut of *Hannie Caulder*. The producers claimed I was in breach of contract, which I wasn't. The only way I could stay out of court and get the money they owe me. What can I tell you?

Arrived in New York and went to the Americana Hotel. I was staying there when John Kennedy was shot. Also went there when I heard about Audie Murphy being killed.

June 2, 1971

Got to London to find they had cut *Hannie Caulder* into a mess. They were about to score it anyway, but I can help it. I've already been offered two scripts in London. Things are looking up.

Recut the picture and they sold it to Paramount within a half an hour.

June 18, 1971

Went back to Hollywood.

July 21, 1971

This is hard to believe, but I'm back in London for the final cut of *Hannie Caulder*. This isn't a picture—it's a way of life.

November 2, 1971

Wrote a new script—*The Train Robbers*. Sent it to Duke Wayne.

December 1971
Made a deal with Duke's son Michael to do *Train Robbers* starring John Wayne. I'm back in business.

Flew to Durango from Burbank in a seven-passenger Navajo. Nate Edwards [Duke's transportation man], George Coleman, Mike Wayne, and a guy who said he was the pilot. Ended up landing in god-awful weather in Mazatlán, then we flew in the storm over mountains with oxygen masks. What can I tell you?

Got to Durango and looked at the location we had already seen. Back to L.A. Christmas.

January 3, 1972
Moved into Warner Bros. Same old joint. Mike Wayne is power-mad. He's young—he'll get over it.

January 8, 1972
Back in Durango. Got sick on Sunday and managed to survive. Went to Torreón to find desert location, which we did. Waiting for Mike Wayne and Al Sweeney, the art director, to join us, so we can get out of Torreón. This is where Ricardo Montalban was born.

January 25, 1972
Went to Newport for a meeting with Wayne. He hasn't changed too much—complains about getting old. And I think he hates his wife. I know *I* do. He had some ideas about the script, some good and some bad.

January 28, 1972
Went to supper with Wayne at the Sportsmen's Lodge. Really an unhappy man, but then again, he likes to complain, He's on the cover of *Life* this week.

January 29, 1972
Went with Wayne to the Motion Picture Center to see Bruce Cabot. Bruce is dying. *Train Robbers* is supposed to go the middle

of March. Wayne seems to be happy, but don't let him fool you. Trying to get Ben Johnson.

Voted for the Academy Awards today. Hard to find five good directors and five good pictures. Ben Johnson will win. Nobody will vote against him because he's not in competition with anybody. Cowboys never are—nor are cowboy writers and directors.

February 24, 1972

Directing a John Wayne picture is like riding a runaway horse with one rein. If you pull too hard the horse falls, and if you let go, *you* fall off.

I have Ann-Margret, Ben Johnson, and Rod Taylor. Picture's supposed to start on the 23rd of March—my lucky day.

February 27, 28, and 29, March 1 and 2, 1972

Duke Wayne arrived in Durango and spent a day with us. Then he went over to his boat in Mazatlán. He invited me to go marlin fishing when we were in L.A., but he forgot about it. I think I'll take the bait out of my luggage.

March 2, 1972

Flew from Durango to Torreón on a private plane, a twin-engine Apache. Call letters on the plane are BUM. Pilot's Mexican. He read the Durango newspaper on the way there. Should have been reading the pilot's manual on how to land. Another air medal—found location and flew back to Durango. Pilot didn't read on the return trip—he slept.

Forgot to mention, when we were coming for a landing, the right engine stopped.

The studio doesn't like the title *The Train Robbers*. I suggested what about *The Wayne Robbers*.

March 9, 1972

Went to have a meeting with a guy named Peter Guber—head of production at Columbia. He was late. He had to go downtown to look at a pinball machine. If you make a bad picture at Columbia, the studio lights up, "Tilt."

He says the town is not too sure of Wayne.

March 12, 1972

Nine A.M.—Met Wayne at his house and drove out to the airport to pick up his jet. A guy served a subpoena on him at the plane, some kind of a divorce action. He didn't deck the guy.

We flew down to Guaymas, and then flew on to Durango—great plane. Duke was in a pretty good mood, but I think he's unhappy at home. Nobody even said good-bye to him when he left.

We're in Durango at the Mexico Courts. We checked in—Duke's asleep in the next room. He asked me to wake him up later. Here's a guy with a million-dollar boat docked over in Mazatlán, a million-dollar plane in the air flying back to L.A., a million-dollar home in Newport Beach, number-one box office in the world, and he's asleep in a lonely, flea-bitten motel room in Durango, Mexico. The room cost $10.40 a night. Beats the hell outta me.

March 15, 1972

Went out riding today with John Wayne. Took two horses from the set and went back into the mountains for about an hour. I rode Wayne's double horse. Best I've ever ridden. He was so good, in fact, Duke traded horses on the way back to Durango.

We start the picture in a week, and I'm ready.

Wayne just had a big fight with his wife on the phone about some tennis courts she wants to buy. Her ex-husband is living here at the Courts with some young chili bean. If Pilar hadn't married Duke, she'd be here in a $10.40-a-day room—makes you think.

My agent called today. He wants to get straightened out how much I owe him.

March 16, 1972

Went riding again with Wayne.

Before I forget it—I'm directing a five-million-dollar picture for Warners, and they have not called me or even acknowledged that I was on the lot. Maybe they're still mad because I walked off *Skin Game*.

When we were coming back from riding, a little boy was sitting alongside the road, crying for a run-over dog. I thought Duke was gonna cry. I did.

March 23, 1972

Wayne cooked steaks last night. This morning we start the picture. I think I've got a chance with this one—hope springs eternal. Plato said, "He who does not take part in government will be ruled by inferiors." Amen.

Started picture today—weather rotten.

April 4, 1972

An eight-year-old Mexican boy was hit by one of our cars on the way to the location this morning. He died. He was deaf, and didn't hear the car coming. I was sick. It doesn't make any sense. I know it could have happened anytime, but right when I think I have life figured out, a thing like this happens. What a terrible thing. I can't help but think I was responsible. I was in a car ahead of them. God must have been looking the other way. Poor baby.

April 6, 1972

Wayne is flying Ann-Margret and Ben Johnson back to L.A. in his jet for the Academy Awards. Nobody thanked me for being three days ahead. Nobody will.

April 10, 1972

Funny thing. Doing a shot on top of a Mexican mountain outside Durango when we heard over the radio that Ben Johnson won the Academy Award. At that very moment, I was shooting a scene with his double, in the rain. Poor Ann-Margret lost to Cloris Leachman. Can't win 'em all.

Finished night's work at twelve-thirty—blew up a tree. Now you know why I don't win awards.

Did a scene today with John Wayne in the rain. He was very good.

April 12, 1972
Ben Johnson came back to work after winning his Academy Award. Poor Ann-Margret, she took her loss pretty hard. By the way, I threw her in the river for her first shot. She'll be all right. It's tough to lose when you're a winner.

August 12, 1972
Finished *The Train Robbers* and spent twelve weeks cutting it. Warners doesn't particularly like it.

✻   ✻   ✻   ✻   ✻

[Looking in the diary I'm skipping two years up until:]

May 15, 1974
I compare today's movie moguls with Frederick the Great's mule. The ass attended as many battles as the king, but never learned anything about war.

✻   ✻   ✻   ✻   ✻

In 1975, Dino De Laurentiis made a deal for me to do a picture, and I remember I wrote in my diary:

"I know how Brigham Young felt when the seagulls came in and ate all the crickets when they were destroying the crops."

And then about three weeks into the picture I got fired, and I wrote in the diary:

"Now I know how Brigham Young would have felt if those seagulls had flown right on by and left him up to his ass in crickets."

✻   ✻   ✻   ✻   ✻

Then on February 17 of 1976, I wrote:

"A man would be a fool to challenge Dino De Laurentiis at this time, when he's considered a giant in the movie industry. I'll wait until they find out what he *really* is—a short Italian."

In September of 1976, I was signed to do a television show, a six-hour *How the West Was Won* with Jim Arness and Bruce Boxleitner. We did it up in Kanab, Utah. It turned out to be very good. As a matter of fact, it probably got one of the highest ratings of any miniseries. It got a 51 share the first night. The second night it got a 49-plus, and then the third night it was a 51-plus again. And that's pretty high, considering the Academy Awards this year, which was very well received, got a 31 share. So anyway, that show was very successful, and it kind of put me back in business.

Then I did a five-hour show down in Mexico called *The Rhineman Exchange*. John Huston worked again for me as an actor, and he wasn't feeling very well, but he did okay in the picture, and he was no problem.

✿   ✿   ✿   ✿   ✿

During the early seventies, I had so many things which didn't work out that most of the entries in the diary were just miserable, so I haven't put them in here. But on May 11, 1992, an entry says:

"Talk about a bad review . . ."

I had done a biopsy because my PSA, which is a test for prostate cancer, was a worrisome 123. I called to get the verdict on what the outcome was and I said to the doctor, "How are you?" And he said, "I'm fine—*you're not*. You've got prostate cancer." Which was not really a shock, because I had been taking tests for about four months, and they hadn't looked good.

I had my operation, what they call a "drastic prostectomy," and it takes about four weeks to get over it. Soon after my recovery, I had a stroke in my right eye, and I lost sight. I can finally park in a handicapped zone, but I can't find it.

6

Music

Irving Thalberg, the young genius who was the head of production at MGM in the thirties, when asked about motion picture music, said, "If it wasn't for music, we'd all be out of business." He was absolutely right.

The music score in a motion picture is probably one of the most important elements of a finished film. It has helped more movies over the years than you can possibly imagine.

Moviegoers are usually not even aware of the score. They don't realize it, but their emotions are being manipulated from one scene to the next. Some of the great ones were Dimitri Tiomkin, Max Steiner, Victor Young, Alfred Newman, Jeff Alexander, Bernard Herrmann, and many more.

I became aware of the importance of music on the first picture I ever did. We were in the dubbing room on a picture called *Seven Men from Now*. There was a scene in a wagon with Lee Marvin, Randolph Scott, and Gail Russell. It was a four-minute scene, and the music composer had written a four-minute, what we call a "cue," as a background to this scene. When we ran the scene with the music, I realized that there was some funny, grim humor in the scene—and the music, which was dramatic, was making it impossible for the audience to laugh at the lines. I realized that the absence of music in some scenes was equally or more important than the music in the scenes where it really belonged.

We ran the scene with the music, and then I said, "Let's do it without the music." We did it, and it worked. That's the way it is in the picture. The composer almost had a heart attack because he'd worked days and days on this four-minute cue. When he saw the finished product, even he realized that it was much better without the music.

Over the years, I've seen rough cuts of pictures before the score has been laid in. One that comes to mind is *The High and the Mighty,* a William Wellman picture that was very successful. I saw a cut of the picture before they had Tiomkin's score, and it was a very good picture, but with the score, it was a great picture.

The same goes for *Treasure of Sierra Madre,* which Max Steiner did. I think he won the Academy Award. Another example is *The Magnificent Seven,* in which a great score by Elmer Bernstein made that picture much better than it was, and I should know, because I did the second *Seven,* and without the score, we'd have been in trouble.

High Noon had a marvelous score. . . . I'm not saying that the score sells the film, but in many cases, it makes it a much more dramatic picture.

When I did *Dirty Dingus Magee* with Frank Sinatra in 1970, he suggested a musician to do the score. This musician had never done a score, so the studio was reluctant. They told me, "Well, if it doesn't work, we'll do it again. It's a lot of money, but we'll do it."

They hired this wonderful guy—he did pop songs, and he was very successful and still is today. Many of the composers farm out some of their work on a picture to other orchestrators. Usually they supervise them to the point where they've almost done the work themselves, but in this case, the morning that the composer got up on the podium and laid the music out in front of him it was very apparent that he'd never seen it before. It wasn't his fault. He got the music at the last minute and couldn't prepare.

We had a huge orchestra of about eighty pieces, which really is too big. Using a mixing board, you can only get so many instruments on a track. He did the score, and it wasn't too good. Actually, it wasn't good at all.

When it was over, I called in a composer I'd used on many pictures, Jeff Alexander, one of the really fine motion picture composers. He never got the credit he should have, but I think every composer in town will agree that he was a tremendous artist. He came in and redid the score and it was just excellent. I felt so sorry for the other composer—not because the score was redone, because that occurred many, many times over the years; it was just that when he got on the podium, it was obvious he'd never seen the music before and it was terrible to see him go through it. I mean, he was sweating bullets. We finally got the picture scored and the composer we replaced went on to bigger and better things.

There is nothing more thrilling than when you've written a script, gone out and shot it, cut it—and then walk out on a music stage and have incredible music bring it completely alive.

I once had a musician come to me, Shelley Manne. He was a drummer. He had an idea to score a picture, a western, with nothing but percussion instruments—drums and bells and all. The orchestra was only about twenty-five guys, and the producer thought it was the greatest idea he'd ever heard because the music would cost only about a third of what it would have naturally cost.

Shelley did the score, and it's quite interesting. It's on a picture I did called *Young Billy Young*, with Bob Mitchum and Angie Dickinson. It's still out there playing on television. I think the only instrument he had to carry any kind of a melody on was a guitar, and maybe a harmonica. The rest was all percussion. It was a little lacking when you got into a big dramatic shoot-out or something, but many people thought it was quite good. (I wasn't one of them.)

I was doing a picture in Spain years ago, and it was suggested that I use a composer named Ken Thorne, a British composer—a fantastic guy, very talented. When I heard his music, I was so taken with him that I thought I had discovered a new talent. Well, it turned out he had won an Academy Award for the music on a picture he'd done about five years before. I'm famous for doing things like that.

My favorite composer was a gentleman I mentioned before, Jeff Alexander. He did *The Rounders, Dirty Dingus Magee,* and a number of other pictures for me. He was just superb. As I said, he never really got the credit he should have, and yet at the Motion Picture Academy, Jeff Alexander was one of the heads of the committee that selects the best scores of the year for the Academy Awards. To a man, every composer I've talked to about Jeff said he knew more about music than almost anyone else on the planet. He also had a great sense of humor that was revealed in both his music and in his use of instruments.

Speaking of instruments, Ken Thorne said an interesting thing. He feels that musicians, as a rule, are drawn to the instruments they go on to play because of their personalities. In other words, the real loud person will wind up in the brass section; very quiet, easygoing people are in the string sections; the nervous fellows focus on percussion; and very quiet, calm people play the French horn, which is known as "the soul of the orchestra."

I'd say without a doubt that the most important element that goes into making a motion picture is the music score. There will be those who disagree, but they're wrong.

7

Greats

Looking back, I've been privileged to know some really great people. It started, I believe, when I was in the Army. I was in Fort Riley, Kansas, and I was introduced to Joe Louis, the heavyweight champion of the world. He was a drill sergeant in an all-black unit at Fort Riley in the summer of '42. A very nice man—gentle, big, and I liked him very much. He only stayed a drill sergeant for a short period of time, and then the Special Services had him teaching boxing. He went around and did exhibition fights. He was a delightful guy.

I was very impressed with him, because they told me that he would throw parties at the noncommissioned officers' club and pay for everything. He'd have all the guys there, and they worshipped him. He was probably the first great I ever met in my life.

Speaking of fighters, later on, Kenny Norton, who was the champ for a while, was working in a picture I was doing in Puerto Rico. He introduced me to Muhammad Ali, and I was very impressed with him. I didn't realize he was so big—he's tall. He's got a good sense of humor—a very nice guy. It's hard to believe that they were such killers in the ring, because he and Louis were two really outstanding guys.

There were other greats I met when I was young. I met General MacArthur in the Philippines. He made a promise. He told the Filipinos "I shall return," and we used to say, "Why did he have to bring us with him?" Actually, I returned two days before he got there—at Leyte.

Later on, when we were in Manila, we went down to free the prisoners in Santo Tomás prison and he flew in on an L-5 Air-Evac plane. He landed out in the street, and my outfit was the honor guard while he came up to give a speech to the prisoners.

A short time later I was in a bombed-out building on Dewey Boulevard in Manila. I was looking out into Manila Bay with field glasses, and somebody tapped me on the shoulder and said, "Give me those glasses."

I said, "Wait a minute," and when I turned around, it was MacArthur, so I about fainted and handed him the glasses. He was a prima donna, but he was a hell of a general. I must say, we made three landings in the Pacific, and every time he put us off in the right place. We didn't get shot at in Leyte, and we didn't get shot at in Luzon. He got a lot of bum raps, but he was a real commander.

Then of course, there was that wonderful speech he made in Congress, about "old soldiers never die, they just fade away." MacArthur could also be funny. He was watching television when Eisenhower was elected President, and his wife said, "Do you think he'll make a good President?"

MacArthur answered, "Well, he was a good company clerk for me."

In the picture business, I met a lot of greats, like John Wayne, John Ford, Wild Bill Wellman, the director Henry Hathaway, who did some of the very best pictures, and Raoul Walsh, who was a real colorful character. He had one eye. He lost the other fighting against Pancho Villa. He was riding with Pancho Villa, or he was chasing after him. Anyway, he was quite a guy, and he made some great pictures too.

Of course, there was Frank Borzage. Frank was a dear man, and he won the first Academy Award, with Bill Wellman, for *Seventh Heaven*. He had three brothers—Danny and Lou, and I don't recall the other one.

I met Gable, and Budd Boetticher, who is a cult figure, and I met Bogart, and Katharine Hepburn.

In 1966, I was doing a picture called *The Money Trap* with Glenn Ford and Joseph Cotten and a few others, at Metro, when Hepburn came on the set with her nephew and asked if she could visit. She told me this was the stage where they had made *The Philadelphia Story*.

She stood around and watched me work. I remember I did a scene with Glenn and Joseph Cotten, and when it was over, I said, "Print," and she said to me, "Are you gonna print *that*?"

I said, "Yes," and she said, "Well, it's your picture." I think she was kidding.

There was Angela Lansbury, who was marvelous. There were Robert Mitchum, Glenn Ford, Kirk Douglas, Yul Brynner, and Jim Garner . . . dear Henry Fonda, who was wonderful, and his kids, Jane and Peter, and then of course, Ernie Borgnine, one of my buddies; Jack Elam, Walter Brennan—a delightful person who was a little to the right of Attila the Hun, but a great guy.

I love the story Walter Brennan told me about working with John Ford. He was having trouble getting on a horse. And Ford yelled at him "Can't you even mount a horse?" And Walter said, "No, but I got three Oscars for acting!"

On the other hand, Ward Bond was a real horse's ass. Whenever you put the camera low and have the riders come through the foreground, where the horses' asses loom in the foreground, that's called a "Ward Bond shot," even to this day. Ward Bond thought he was God's gift to the ladies. But in fact, if a woman had got Ward as a gift, she'd have returned him.

Rita Hayworth, who was a delight; Raquel Welch, who was Raquel Welch; Ann-Margret, a dear girl; and my love, Angie Dickinson, whom I've known for probably thirty-five or forty years, and who is sensational.

I worked with Lauren Hutton, who's a beautiful gal . . . and Ginger Rogers, who was probably in her fifties at the time, and was still very beautiful.

Joel McCrea and Randy Scott and Lee Marvin, who ended up not liking me, and I don't know why, because I've always thought he was one of the great, great actors. He was in the first script I ever did, *Seven Men from Now.*

Gene Tierney, whom I met in the Army, and Sally Rand, the fan dancer.

My dear friend Ben Johnson; Claire Trevor, who at eighty-eight is still a dynamite lady; Harry Carey Jr., another dear friend; Frank Sinatra; and Clint Eastwood.

Audie Murphy, my hero . . .

Another hero was Neil Armstrong. He came onto the set and had his picture taken with Suzanne Pleshette, Gene Evans, and Jim Garner, from *Support Your Local Gunfighter.* Later I met Buzz Aldrin.

Oh, one gal I forgot—Susan Hayward. I wanted to use her in *Welcome to Hard Times,* but it didn't work out. When I first met her, it was the initial day of the shooting of *Seven Men from Now,* out at the Warners ranch.

An actor by the name of Don Red Berry, who was dating Susan at the time, brought her out to the set, and he took me over to introduce me to her. She looked at me and said, "Burt, do you have any idea how many paper bags are used in Los Angeles in one day? I'm giving up the picture business and going into the paper bag business." That was my introduction to Susan Hayward.

The same kind of thing happened to me when I was introduced to Jackie Gleason. He was rehearsing a show on Broadway and my friend Jim Hennigan took me backstage. I remember at the end of the second act, he took me out onstage and introduced me to Gleason, and he said, "Burt Kennedy, this is Jackie Gleason," and Jackie turned to me, and he said, "I'm gonna be a *smash* in this show."

It was *Ah! Wilderness,* and he *was* a smash in the show.

*   *   *   *   *

When the western movies dried up in the seventies, I turned to television. Although I fooled around in it some in the very beginning of my Hollywood career, I never even watched television, but I decided that in order to keep the money coming in, I would do it.

The first show that I did was *Seven Brides for Seven Brothers.* It was a series based on the picture. The first TV executive I ever met was at Metro. He was the head of television there, David Gerber. I was taken up to his office and when the secretary let me in he was behind the desk on the phone. He was wearing a chicken suit, the reason being that there was a sequence in the show where the seven boys dressed up like chickens. David was checking out the chicken outfit; he was a "hands-on" producer.

I had a story conference with this guy sitting behind his desk in a chicken outfit. It had a beak and a big comb—it was the damnedest thing I'd ever seen. And he was very serious. He thought the beak was too long, and he just wanted to check out everything with the wardrobe department.

That was my first venture into series television after my motion picture career.

I went on then to do a show over at Warner Bros. called *Yellow Rose,* with Sam Elliott and Cybill Shepherd. It didn't stay on the air, but it was a good show. Sam's very good. He's found his niche in television westerns. He's excellent.

I'm really glad I did television. It is a big mistake for writers, directors and actors to sit around and wait for a picture to come along. As Will Rogers told Joel McCrea many years ago, "Quit complaining about the material just keep working."

Henry Hathaway used to say, "Stay on salary. No matter what, stay on salary."

Which reminds me of my early days, and could be encouragement for those people out there trying to break into the writing business. I went with an agency named Stewart and Stewart. Only there were *three* Stewarts. There was Lee Stewart, Rosalie Stewart, and another one. Rosalie was quite famous. She had handled George Kelly on Broadway and was a very savvy gal.

I had written some scripts, and she took them around. One day she called me—this was after about a year—and said, "Burt, it isn't worth the gasoline I use to drive around trying to sell your scripts, so I can't handle your stuff anymore."

The very next day, I signed a contract with John Wayne, and I was under contract for the next ten years. Rosalie said she was sorry, but she'd lost a lot of money on me. So any of you new young writers out there who are struggling, just remember, success could be around the next corner.

I love the thing that happened when I was a student at the Pasadena Playhouse. They had a graduation ceremony one year, and they asked an actor named Tom Powers to speak at it. He said, "I'll speak, if I can say anything I want to." They said sure, fine.

He walked out on the stage, facing the students. There must have been five hundred of them down in front, plus the faculty up in the balcony. He said, "Before I start, I want to tell you students something that you should always keep in mind." He said, "Look up there in the balcony. Those are your instructors, your teachers." He continued, "You shouldn't pay a lot of attention to what they say, because if any one of them could get a job in professional theater, they wouldn't be here." After the big groan from the balcony, he went on and gave his speech. It was good advice.

A lot of good actors came from the Playhouse. Robert Preston, who was one of my favorite actors, graduated from the Playhouse, as did Victor Jory. That's going back a ways, but he was a great heavy, a great actor. Edgar Buchanan, who didn't start acting until he was in his late fifties. He was a dentist before that. There were a number of others.

The first thing I ever wrote was a live television show at Knott's Berry Farm out here in Buena Park. We had a cowboy named Jim Bannon, and the gag was we were going to do a rodeo. The problem was that the rodeo grounds were about a block away from where they had a western street, and they wanted to start the show with this cowboy star riding in up the street. He pulls up and gets off his horse, and he says, "My name is so-and-so, and I want to welcome you to the so-and-so Rodeo Days." He gets back up on his horse and rides out.

We only had one camera, so what we did was put the camera in a pickup truck. When the cowboy got back up on the horse and rode out, we started the truck and we beat him over to the rodeo grounds. When we got back from the live commercial we planned to pick him up coming through the front gate, and in that way we'd do the rodeo with only one camera.

The problem was that when we went back to the studio for the first commercial—it was the Pacific Fence Company, I'll never forget—they weren't ready. As we sent it back to them, they were moving the fence, and this worker was backing up, with his rear end in the camera. They had a section of the fence with the word PACIFIC on it, and they stumbled through it.

Unfortunately, the sponsor was watching, and called right away. We were canceled between the western street and the rodeo grounds, but we didn't know it. We went on and did the show. For nothing, as it turned out, because our sponsor wouldn't pay us.

I remember another time over at KLAC, on Cahuenga Boulevard in Hollywood. I had written a show, and after the second act we had to change the sets. So we opened the stage door, which went right out on Cahuenga, and the crew took all the sets and put them out into the street.

These sets, in the middle of Cahuenga, stopped all traffic. People were blowing their horns and raising hell, but we got the other set up and closed the doors and kept going on with our show. I'm sure in New York they can tell even bigger horror stories about live television, but that was mine. I got out of it. Too nerve-wracking.

Even on film, television can be rough. I remember I was doing a show at Warner Bros. years ago. It was a series called *The Lawman*, with John Russell and Peter Brown. In television, you shoot, rain or shine.

We were out on the back lot in a driving rainstorm. It was raining hard, with thunder and lightning. When you took hold of the wheels of the camera, you'd get this tremendous jolt. I'm not sure where the shock was coming from, but I assume it was from all the cables lying in the water. It damn near knocked you off the dolly. The operator had to wear big rubber gloves so he could operate without getting electrocuted.

Speaking of being electrocuted, I was doing *The Deserter* in Rome, and we were shooting a scene which was supposed to take place during a thunderstorm. The way you make lightning is you take two electrical cables and put them on what we call "scissors," which are just long poles that are bolted together at the bottom. Then, when you want to have lightning, you pull these poles together, like a pair of scissors, and when the two arcs get close enough, the spark will jump from one to the other and give off blue flame.

So we were doing this thing onstage in Rome, and I said to the effects man, "Are you gonna use scissors?"

He said, "Oh, yes, yes." They always told you what you wanted to hear in Italy.

We got going, and all of a sudden I heard thunder, and it's time for the lightning, and I looked up to see an electrician. He had on a pair of dark goggles, and instead of having the scissors on the boards, he had these two cables in his hands, which he held out in front of him until they sparked. He was standing in the rain doing this!

I stopped everything and said, "You can't do that! Get scissors!"

The effects man argued, "No, those are too dangerous."

I insisted, "But the guy could be killed!"

He tried to assure me, "No, no, we do this all the time." They may still be doing it. I don't know.

❖   ❖   ❖   ❖   ❖

On another occasion I was doing a *Combat* episode and the gag was that this ambulance was stuck in the mud. We were doing it on a stage, with pouring rain, lightning, and thunder. Vic Morrow and the others on the show were trying to push this ambulance out. The driver would gun it, they would push, and then there was all this rain and lightning.

I got everything all screwed up, and I called "Action," and here all the lightning was going, and the rain, and then the truck was spinning its wheels and mud was flying all over the place. When it was over, I said, "Great," and the soundman said, "No, it's not great, we never rolled the camera." We did it over again, and it was even better.

One of the problems with being a director is that you probably make four hundred decisions in a day, little things. People come up and ask, do you want this, do you want that.

Sometimes an actor would come up and say, "Am I finished?"

Not thinking, I'd say, "Yeah."

And they'd ask, "Can I go home?"

And I'd say, "Fine."

On this one occasion I was in Spain shooting *The Deserter,* on a location called El Torcal, north of Málaga. We were up in these mountains. Richard Crenna and Ricardo Montalban were doing a scene. It was late in the day, and Richard came up to me when I was busy and said, "Are you through with me? Can I go home?"

I said, "Yes."

Later, when we were getting ready to do this scene, we got the camera set up and all of a sudden I realized I'd sent Crenna home. Luckily, by the time they got it lit, it started to rain, and when it was raining hard enough, I just said, "All right, that's a wrap. Let's go home." Nobody ever knew that I had goofed.

I take that back. I'm sure Crenna did, because he's a good director himself and I suspect he was trying to pull one. I never did ask him, but I will one day.

✻ ✻ ✻ ✻ ✻

The scariest location I was ever on was during a picture I did in a coal mine, where there was a cave-in and a bunch of people were caught in it.

When we were looking for a coal mine for *Big Bad John,* we flew to Knoxville, Kentucky, and drove to a little town where a mine was located. In order for us to go down and look at the mine, we had to take a "safety" class. It took about two hours; we had to wear a certain kind of shoe, and we had to wear helmets with lights on them. We had this gear we had to learn to use in case there was a fire in the mine.

When anything happens in a mine, the first thing that goes out are the lights. You have to learn to put on a mask and start the oxygen in the dark. The instructors put us in a room and turned off the lights, and they said, "All right now, put your mask on." You have to learn to do it, or they won't let you down in the mine.

After all of that, we looked at that mine, and it wasn't good for us. We ended up in Trinidad, Colorado. You didn't go down in the ground in an elevator. These were mines where they tunneled straight into the base of the mountain. This tunnel went back in under the mountain about a mile.

We went into this mine. Now, as you get farther into the mine, the ceiling seems to get lower, until finally the whole mountain is right on top of your head. You have to duck down; it's amazing. You think about it and you feel the weight of the whole mountain on you. They had it propped up with timbers but it was really scary. It was the scariest place I ever worked. And to keep you on your toes, every once in a while a big chunk of rock would come down and hit you on the head or on the shoulder, just to remind you that there was movement all the time.

I had to do some scenes in there. I guess we spent about four or five days in that damn mine. It was like working in a submarine (which I've never done, and don't want to).

There was a big scene where there were timbers crashing, which was all special effects. I thought, I can't do that back here, five hundred feet into this mountain. What if something really goes wrong? I decided to do the scene right at the entrance— that was the highest part of the mine anyway.

We were able to rig up all our fake timbers and we did the cave-in. I guess it was good, because we had used some of the real miners as extras, and when we did the scene, some of them came to me and said, "I was in a cave-in once, and it wasn't near that bad." Again, that was the scariest location I ever worked on.

As it turned out, as usual when you work very hard and take chances, the damn picture wasn't too good. There was so much stuff done in the mine, I suggested to the front office that they should take canaries in cages down in the front rows when they previewed the picture, and if the canaries died, they should get the hell out.

✧   ✧   ✧   ✧   ✧

A picture in a mine that I *didn't* do . . . I was in London, and I was coming back to L.A. for some reason. I read in the paper that the little pit ponies who pulled coal cars in the mines in Wales were being replaced with mechanical trains. These ponies were born, lived, and died down in the mines. They were born blind and they were blind their whole life. Their next destination was a slaughterhouse.

I thought this would be a great premise for a movie about how some kids try to save the ponies. It turns out that there's a big fire in the mine. The ponies know their way around in the dark mines and are able to lead the miners out and save their lives— it's a good story.

I wrote it down and I took it to Disney. The head of Disney at the time was a fellow named Ron Miller, who used to be a football player, I think at UCLA or USC. He had married Disney's daughter. I was called and they said, "We want to talk to you about this story."

I went over to Disney, and Ron Miller, who was very nice, and another story man came in. They said, "We really love this story, but it's not your cup of tea."

I said, "I wrote it."

They said, "Yeah, but you don't do this kind of a picture, you do westerns."

I had no choice but to sell them the story for very little money. As it turned out, the reason they didn't want me to do it was that they had an existing deal with a wonderful British writer—I forget her name, but she had done *Upstairs, Downstairs*. They didn't have any material for her, so they gave her this material. Then they brought in a British director to direct it, Charles Jarrott. It seems he had a deal with Disney too, so they turned my project over to them, and they did it. It's called *The Littlest Horse Thieves*. It's pretty good—not as good as it should have been, but it's pretty good.

Jarrott went on to direct one of the worst pictures I've ever seen, the remake of *Lost Horizon*. It wasn't his fault.

But those things happen. I remember one time a writer named Harry Templeton wrote a book, and they gave it to me over at Warner Bros. I read it, and I thought it'd make a real good movie, so I sent it to a guy named Walter McKuen, who was third man in control.

I never heard from him. And about three months later I was over there doing a script for Laurence Harvey and a writer came into my office and said, "I'm Harry Templeton, and I've been brought out here to do the screenplay of my book."

The name of the book was *Ride Out the Night*—a good story, a murder mystery in the West. The studio brought Harry out, he did a version of it, and then they hired someone else to do another version. They never even thanked me for finding it. It was really a good piece of material, which they never made. They did a series from it, using the characters: *The Lawman*. That's happened to me a couple of times in this business, where I find something and somebody else makes it.

Which reminds me: I can't remember names. I was doing a script at Warners again, and a fellow named Tom Gaddis wrote a book called *The Birdman of Alcatraz*, the life story of a criminal named Robert Stroud. When Gaddis came to the writers' building at Warners to start work on the script, writer Guy Trosper, my dear friend, brought him into my office and introduced me to him.

When he left, my secretary came in, and I introduced Tom Gaddis as Robert Stroud. The secretary left the room, and Gaddis said, "No, I'm Tom Gaddis—Robert Stroud was the Birdman of Alcatraz."

So I later said to my secretary, "I'm sorry, when I introduced you to Robert Stroud, it wasn't Robert Stroud. He's the Birdman of Alcatraz and that was Tom Gaddis, the writer."

She said, "That's okay. You introduced me as the leading lady of the script you're writing."

＊   ＊   ＊   ＊   ＊

John Wayne was the same way—he couldn't remember names. He called me Fred for about two years when I first went with him. He kind of had an excuse for that, because Fred Kennedy was one of John Ford's stuntmen, who he used in all his pictures. He later was killed, and died in John Ford's arms on a picture called *The Horse Soldiers*. He had done a very simple saddle fall off a horse, and hit the wrong way. Ford knew immediately that something was wrong and ran to him, and held him in his arms until he died.

Ford was never the same about stunts after that. Never the same about the picture business either.

Another name story: I was doing a script for *The Tall T*. Wayne had a publicity man who was right out of *What Makes Sammy Run?* The story about casting for the picture was on the front pages of both the *Reporter* and *Variety*, and they had my name spelled wrong—Bert.

I arrived at work, and as I came through the door, the publicity man met me. He was all excited, and he said, "Burt, I know they spelled your name wrong in both stories, but the thing was, I was talking to Hedda Hopper, and Louella Parsons, and the boys at the trade papers, and I was in a hurry. They spelled your name wrong, but it'll never happen again, Jim." So after being "Fred" for two years at Wayne's company, I was "Jim" for another two years. But in those days, as long as they were paying me, I didn't care what they called me.

Going on with the name game . . . the Los Angeles Critics Association asked me to their yearly awards luncheon a couple of years ago. I was asked to present a lifetime achievement award to Budd Boetticher, the director. I accepted. The luncheon was at a fancy hotel ballroom.

Clint Eastwood and a number of other dignitaries, including all of the nominees for an Academy Award that year attended. I looked at the program, and it said that the award was going to be presented to Budd Boetticher by Burt Young. I mentioned this to Kevin Thomas, a critic for the *Los Angeles Times* who was there—and who, by the way, is one of the nicest people in the whole world. He got ahold of Charles Champlin, who was the event's emcee, and pointed out the goof on the name.

Champlin got up and said, "We're sorry, but in your program the lifetime achievement award for Budd Boetticher is going to be presented not by Burt Young, but by Burt Kennedy."

When it came time to give my speech, I told my story about when I went to Oklahoma with a picture of mine, in a little town called Grove, and I took my two daughters. When the picture was over, they had me up on the stage to sign autographs. The picture was *The War Wagon* with John Wayne and Kirk Douglas.

I signed autographs, and when they'd gone, my little daughter Bridget, who was seven at the time, came up to me, and she said, "Dad, how come you're famous out in the country and nobody knows you in town?"

So they laughed, and then I said, "Now, thanks to the Los Angeles Critics Association, they know me in town as Burt Young."

It seems the only ones who don't have a problem remembering my name are the Internal Revenue Service agents. It keeps you from getting overconfident.

I remember one time we were having a wrap party on a picture I'd finished over at Metro and we were all having drinks and talking. The craft service man—a glorified janitor who cleans up the set—was at the party. He had a couple of drinks. He came over to me at the bar, and he said, "Mr. Kennedy, I have been in the picture business for fifty years, and I have worked with some of the greatest directors in this town. I don't mind telling you, you're more than adequate."

I thanked him and had another drink.

✿   ✿   ✿   ✿   ✿

Changing the subject, but there was a big splash of news about two producers in Hollywood who took Sony for a financial ride, Peter Guber and Jon Peters. I want to read you what I put in my diary the day that Sony made their deal. Sony paid them an outrageous sum, in the millions, to take over the production of their company, and I wrote down: *"These are two of the biggest bombs that have been dropped on Japan since Hiroshima and Nagasaki."*

8

Location

Hunting

If I'd been paid ten cents a mile for all the time I've spent in a plane, on a train, in a car, or on foot looking for locations for movies, I'd be rich. Let's just take one film at random—*The Rounders*.

We started off by flying to Tucson. Marty Ritt had just finished *Hombre* down there with Paul Newman, Marty Balsam and others. It was from the Elmore Leonard novel. Someone at the studio said, "Boy, those locations are perfect for *Rounders*."

We got to Tucson and got in our cars. We had the art director, the construction man, and the cameraman, the usual entourage. We went out to this location where Marty had shot part of his western, some thirty miles from town. It was about a hundred and ten degrees and completely miserable.

We got out there, and it wasn't going to work at all. Whoever had offered this suggestion hadn't read the script. We stayed about four days in Tucson, running around, and except for the old town street, which we didn't need, none of the locations worked at all.

So we got on a plane and flew up to Phoenix. Somebody said they had built a soundstage and a western street there.

They had built a street—the worst street I'd ever seen. They had a stage, which was fine, but didn't work for our picture. We spent three days roaming around, and we finally said this isn't going to work.

Then somebody came up with a bright idea: Why not shoot it in town? It was a lot cheaper—we wouldn't have to take people on location. We went back to Los Angeles and went out to the Valley, with its brown grass and smoggy skies. Just awful. We threw that out after about two days of running around and got back on a plane.

All this time, I kept saying, "Why don't we go to Sedona?" The art director said, "No, that's no good—it's all been shot before."

We spent another two weeks going all over the place. We ended up in Santa Fe, New Mexico, and checked into a wonderful hotel, the La Fonda. This was in 1964, and I stayed in a room that cost $11.50 a night. Recently, I went back there, and the same room cost $215 a night. That's progress, I guess.

We went up there, touring around and looking at all the locations. There was a wonderful man named Ralph Ives who had built part of a western street out on his ranch. We went out and looked at it; it was not good. He later built a big street out there. (I had told him to wait until someone had a big picture to make, and to let them build the street for him, which he did, and he later rented that street out to many productions.)

It was beautiful in Santa Fe, but after three days of running around, I said, "Let's go to Sedona."

There was no way to get to Sedona except to fly into Flagstaff and take cars down the Oak Creek Canyon into Sedona. In those days, it was a beautiful place. Duke had shot *The Angel and the Badman* there many years before—in black and white, by the way. Duke, dear Gail Russell, and Harry Carey. A good picture. It's in the public domain, so now you see it on television all the time, because nobody has to pay anything for it.

We arrived in Sedona, and within an hour we found every location we needed within a radius of a half an hour. There were
rodeo grounds; a fish hatchery; the main street, which was beautiful—everything we needed. There had been a hundred pictures
made in Sedona, Arizona and *The Rounders* was the first picture
in which Sedona was called by its real name. The picture's so
beautiful that I wouldn't be surprised if it had a lot to do with
the fact that today there's a main highway running through the
town. They've just ruined it, but it's still a beautiful spot. In those
days, it was even more so.

After three weeks of running around all these different places,
we ended up in Sedona, and that's where we made the picture.

✢ ✢ ✢ ✢ ✢

My next picture, *Return of the Seven,* which was the sequel to
The Magnificent Seven, had to be shot in Spain. We were in the
right country, but it took us about four weeks driving all over hell
to find where we wanted to build our various sets and shoot the
picture.

We went to Málaga, all up and down the Costa del Sol—and
we ended up in Alicante, which is a beautiful little seaport.

Now, everyone who had been going over there had been shooting in Almería, so we went there first. Almería was great in that
there were a couple of western streets and a great desert location
just outside of town where David Lean shot much of *Lawrence
of Arabia.* I was to later come back there many times, but on this
occasion I passed on Almería and went up to Alicante, which is
farther up the coast.

We had two villages to build; we found the location to build
them about twenty miles outside of town. Actually, that wasn't
too painful, except that in those days the flights from Madrid to
Alicante were pretty hairy, in that you flew down in a C-47, which
is a great airplane but was about forty years old at the time. There
were no cement runways in those days. The pilots would land
these 47s on one wheel so that in case one tire blew, they still
had one left.

I remember the first flight we took. I was with my first assistant, Pepe Lopez. He hated to fly. When we were coming in over the coast, there were big cliffs. The heat makes an updraft, and as we came over this cliff, we must have dropped five hundred feet. The pilot was sitting in the seat behind me with a stewardess, and the copilot was flying the plane. The pilot was trying to get up to the cockpit, and he had to crawl. There was such a G-force it was just pushing him down into the floor. But it's pretty hard to wreck one of those 47s. Poor Pepe never flew again.

In those days, I never went anywhere that I didn't have my seat belt on, but Pepe had taken his off, and he went up to the ceiling, and I grabbed him. Everything on the plane came off. They had curtains on the windows and they all came off, all the silverware went flying everywhere, and people were screaming. But we landed, and found the locations within a short period of time, so that was relatively painless.

On the trip we took to find the locations for *Drum*, the sequel to the successful *Mandingo*, we went to New York, then Jamaica and Cartagena, and ended up shooting ten minutes from my house down here on Coldwater Canyon. On that one, we must have traveled a good twenty-five thousand miles, at least, to find something ten minutes from my house. I never finished *Drum*, due to a knock-down, drag-out fight with Dino.

❖   ❖   ❖   ❖   ❖

The Good Guys and the Bad Guys was to be made in New Mexico. Again, we were back in Santa Fe. We needed a railroad, and the location manager told us about this place—Chama, New Mexico, the end of the line for a railroad that ran from up in Colorado. I later used that same railroad on another picture, and it was perfect for us. In the fall Chama is probably the most beautiful spot of anyplace I've ever been.

We had to fly into Chama with an Aero Commander and we landed in a field where the weeds were about four feet high. When we got out of the plane, I said we deserved to get air medals.

It was in Chama that I came up with an idea that I've used many times in looking for locations. Because most of the story was set near a railroad, we had to find various places to build stations. Rather than lug everybody around on a full train, I got one of those hand-motor cars which hold four or five people. We would take the motor putt-putt and go up the track until we found a spot that was good for the location. I used it again on *The Train Robbers*. I've used it four or five times and it really is a time-saver.

We were going to headquarter in Chama. The problem with Chama was that there wasn't enough lodging for our crew. It was a big picture, and we had a hundred and fifty people with us. My friend Bill Finnegan was the production manager and we went through the problems that you always do when you go to look at a location—nothing seems right. Except, in this case, the railroad was number one, so that made our decision. We had to shoot it there.

Everybody in the group was saying, "Well, this is a bad location. There's no place to eat, there's no place to sleep," and so on. This happens on just about every picture and you finally have a meeting. I used to say, "Okay, fellas, to begin with, we're gonna make the picture here. Now let's figure out how we can make it work."

Once you say that, once the decision is made, for some reason, the problems start getting solved. In the case of Chama, Bill Finnegan decided that he would keep part of the crew in Chama and the rest in a nearby fishing camp.

Then he came up with the idea about feeding. There was one restaurant in town by the railroad station, but it was too small. So Bill, who was great at organization, decided to take over the gymnasium of the school and feed everybody there. We fended for ourselves during the day, but at night, we would all meet at this place, and we'd have a kitchen crew from the picture cook the evening meal.

After the second night, nobody came to the gymnasium to eat. They all found their own ways of doing things. For example, they caught fish and cooked them on grills at the lodges. It was amazing. We all took care of ourselves, and it really worked. After we shot up there, and people saw how beautiful it was, there were a number of pictures made in Chama. I even went back twice myself.

For *The War Wagon* we went to Durango, where Duke had done many shows. I had seen a picture called *The Tall Man*, with Clark Gable, which had been shot in this beautiful location, and I went to Columbia Studios to find out where it was. It was called Los Organos, it was about eighty-five miles from Durango, and it was beautiful.

We went to Durango, got in a car, and drove to Los Organos. Now, part of the time we were on dirt roads, going through little Mexican villages and so on, and the farther we went, the grimmer Duke looked, and he kept saying, "Burt, do you really want to shoot this far away from Durango, with all these man-hours?"

By the time we got to Los Organos, Duke was fit to be tied. When you come upon Los Organos, you come around a corner to a beautiful panoramic view. It's almost like you're in the bottom of the Grand Canyon—and all these gorgeous rocks that look like organs. That's why they're called that, I suppose. As soon as Duke saw it, he gasped, "Oh, my God! We've *gotta* shoot here!"

As soon as he decided that we were going to shoot there, people started saying, "We could build an airport, and we could get a C-47, and we could bring the crew up in the morning, and it's only a ten-minute flight. . . ."

That's what we did. We built an airport, and we got a C-47, and every morning when we were working in Los Organos, we flew up on one of two flights. One was the beer flight, which was so early the pilot would taxi down to the end of the runway, and when it got light enough so that he could see the fence at the other end of the strip, he would take off. Once there, he'd dump us off, fly back, land, and bring the champagne flight, which was all the actors and various other people who wanted to sleep in an extra hour. We did that through the whole picture. Some of the people went up in cars. Emilio Fernandez, the great Mexican director and actor (he was Mapache in *The Wild Bunch*), refused to fly with a Mexican pilot, so he drove up every morning with the group of people who also preferred not to fly.

Speaking of Los Organos, I always wanted to build a western street in that area, but it was always too expensive, even on big pictures with Wayne. It wasn't until I was doing a television movie for Hanna-Barbera that I was able to figure out how to build a street up there. What we did was prefab the buildings in Durango, take them out there on trucks, and put them up. I think there were about seven. The picture was *Shootout in a One-Dog Town*, with Dick Crenna, Stefanie Powers, Jack Elam, Gene Evans, Richard Egan, and a number of the old gang. That was the only time I really got to use Los Organos the way I wanted to. I went back on *The Train Robbers*. We also did some second-unit trek shots there.

It was a hellish location to get to. I mean, you'd work all day and if you didn't make the champagne flight coming back, you'd have to return in a car. We'd get back to Durango after dark, have a drink, and go to bed exhausted. Making westerns is tough.

The worst, or the most time-consuming, and the most tiring, was trying to find the locations for *The Deserter* for Dino De Laurentiis. We went to Spain, where the picture was eventually shot. We had to go to a location outside of Málaga, up in the mountains, El Torcal. It was a murderous location, two hours from the hotel.

The problem with finding locations on that picture was that we would find something, and then we'd get a call from De Laurentiis, and he'd say, "Look, I've made a coproduction deal with Yugoslavia, and I'm sending a plane over there for you to go take a look at the locations around Dubrovnik and Split."

He sent in a plane, and we got in the plane and flew to Dubrovnik (where they recently had that hellish plane crash that killed Secretary of Commerce Ron Brown). We got to Dubrovnik, which is a very picturesque seaside town in Yugoslavia. But there wasn't any area for the big open battle scenes we had in the picture. So we got in cars and drove up the Dalmatian coast. That's quite a trip along the Adriatic, up to Split, and then on up into Zada. In Zada, we drove into the mountains, and on the top of the mountains there were these big, beautiful meadows, which were perfect for the picture.

On the way up to this, there were switchback roads that went up into the mountain, alongside the road on the cliff-side, where the road dropped off about two or three thousand feet. There were huge cement blocks, like a fence, but they were every ten feet. They were ten feet high and four feet thick.

I kept seeing them on the way up there, and I said to somebody, "What are those?"

They said, "There's a terrible wind that comes up into the mountains in the fall, and it could blow trucks off the mountain if these big blocks of cement were not there." I asked them when these winds occurred, and it turned out it was exactly when we were planning to be there to shoot. I decided that was a bad idea.

We got back on our plane and flew to Alicante, where we eventually shot most of the picture. But every time Dino would get a coproduction deal with some country we were back on a plane and going to that country.

First to Yugoslavia, then Italy. That wasn't right, so finally we went back to where we finally made the picture, Almería, Spain. That was the first of four pictures I did in Almería.

We totaled a lot of miles on that one before we found out what we were doing. These wild-goose chases weren't always to make motion pictures. Some of them happened during television shoots, such as a show I did called *Where the Hell's That Gold?*

We had to have a railroad again, so I went back to Chama. It was decided that it would be too expensive to work out of there, so I flew to Spain: to Madrid, to Granada, and from Granada to Cornique. That was the train that Steven Spielberg had used in one of his Indiana Jones pictures.

It was funny. I got out, and the engine had been sitting there so long that there was grass growing out of the tender. It hadn't been run in years, but they said, "There's no problem, we can get this thing running." I thought, No way.

I got on the plane and I flew back to the States. Now, by this time, the producers were really mad at me, because the Spanish production manager had told them the Spanish train was perfect. Now I was the bad guy. I told them, "We might as well go back to Chama—that's the train we have to use."

We ended up using that train. That's the one where I blew up the trestle, and the trestle caught fire and burned up. I was known in New Mexico as "the bridge-burner."

Speaking of trains, one of the best deals I ever pulled was on *Young Billy Young*, with Bob Mitchum, Angie Dickinson, David Carradine, and Bobby Walker Jr. We had to have a train at the opening of the picture, a Mexican train with a bunch of Mexican soldiers on it. The train in Old Tucson wasn't working; the boiler had blown up or something. We went to a place up outside of Florence, Arizona, where there's a stretch of track that was used on *How the West Was Won*.

There's a copper-mining town at the end of the track where the train originates. We went there and met the owner of this copper mine. He didn't have time to talk to us right then, but he said he'd be down in Tucson for a couple of days, so we waited for him. He got to Tucson and was a nice young guy. We were all sitting around drinking, and he got a little crocked and said, "Well, what are you gonna do with the train?"

We told him, and he said, "Well, you can have the train. We don't have the cars—you'll have to bring them in. We only have cars for the copper. But if you bring in the rolling stock that you need, you can use the engine and that stretch of track."

When we got down to how much it was going to cost us, he said, "Well, what the hell, I'll give it to you for nothing." So we said fine, and we used the train. Later he didn't remember that he had made a no-money deal and he was a little put-out, but he went along and the train worked great.

On the subject of money, when we did *The Good Guys and the Bad Guys* we made a deal with the Denver and Rio Grande Railroad. We went into their headquarters and quickly realized they didn't like the picture business. They didn't like it at all, so they gave us a figure that they thought was going to close us out: It would cost $50,000 to use the train.

We gave them the $50,000, and we got the train for four weeks, or whatever it was. We're shooting the picture, Robert Mitchum and George Kennedy are there, and the executive who had made us the deal came on the set with his wife and a couple of the railroad people. I introduced them to Mitchum and to George and we had lunch. When the luncheon was over, the executive said to me, "You know, I wouldn't have walked across the street to see Bob Mitchum. I just don't like doing business with motion picture people." I thought he was going to say, "Now that I've met Mitchum and you guys, though, everything's fine," but he said, "And I still feel the same way."

I don't know what it is about trains, but I did five pictures in a row on trains. I got to meet a lot of railroaders. On *Concrete Cowboys* we were down in Nashville and we had to do business with the head honcho of the railroad, Colonel Somebody.

I went to his office with my production manager and Ray Marsh, my assistant. As soon as we got inside and sat down, he said, "Well, let me be very honest with you. I don't want anything to do with the picture business because they come down here and talk me into using trains, and then they don't do what they say they're going to do, and it's just not worth it to us to do it."

I was sitting there looking at the guy, and I asked, "What were you a colonel in?"

He said, "The cavalry."

"I was in the First Cavalry."

He said, "You're kidding!"

It turned out that he wasn't in the First Cavalry, but he was cavalry, recon, and we had been in the Philippines in practically the same spots—in Cabanatuan, Manila, and a few other places. He knew a lot of the officers that I knew, such as Jim Sparer and General Chase. We got to telling war stories and when it ended up, he said, "How many trains do you want and where do you want 'em?"

Not only did he give us the trains, he came down and personally ran the show. So it pays to have been in the cavalry. But I don't know why the railroaders dislike the picture people so much, because we're all so wonderful.

I did a television show called *Once Upon a Texas Train*. At the opening of the picture I needed a train that pulled into a station out in the country, where there is a big shoot-out. I'd heard there was a train in Ely, Nevada. I'd already shot all the rest of the picture, so I drove up to Ely and got in touch with this fellow who was in charge of the train.

Me at age twenty-three. Photo courtesy of the author.

My discovery. Photo courtesy of the author.

Top: Old Fooler, the only star
I ever discovered. Photo
reprinted by permission of
Turner Entertainment Co.

Inset: Old Fooler, my star.
Photo courtesy of the author.

Bottom: "Censored." *The
Rounders,* 1964, M.G.M.
Photo reprinted by per-
mission of Turner
Entertainment Co.

Left: Mexican vacation, 1966. Photo courtesy of the author.

Center: Casey Tibbs, world champion bronc rider, presenting me with the Cowboy Hall of Fame Award for *War Wagon.* Photo courtesy of the author.

Bottom: Wrap party for *War Wagon* in Mexico City. John Wayne, Kirk Douglas and me. Photo reprinted by permission of Michael Wayne and Universal.

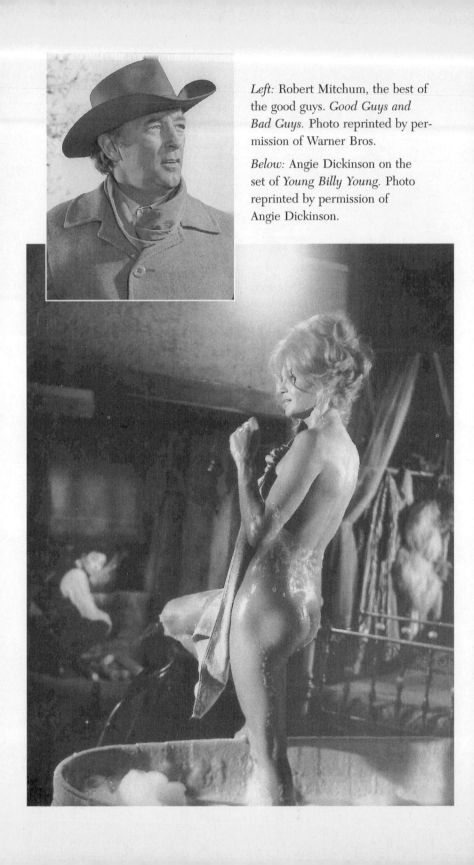

Left: Robert Mitchum, the best of the good guys. *Good Guys and Bad Guys.* Photo reprinted by permission of Warner Bros.

Below: Angie Dickinson on the set of *Young Billy Young.* Photo reprinted by permission of Angie Dickinson.

"I've got a saddle older than you are." *Train Robbers,* 1972. Photo reprinted by permission of Warner Bros.

How the West Was Won. Photo courtesy of the author.

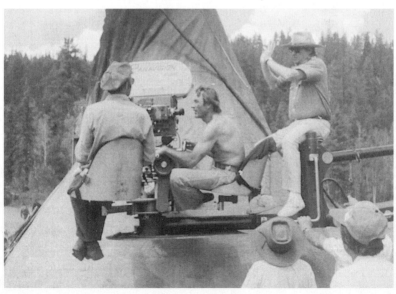

With Tommy Lasorda on the set of *Simon and Simon*. Photo courtesy of the author.

Alec Baldwin and I on the set of *The Alamo*. Photo courtesy of the author.

Harry *M°A°S°H* Morgan at my first annual seventieth birthday party.
Photo courtesy of the author.

Rod Steiger and I on the set of *Wolf Lake*. Photo courtesy of
the author.

Once Upon a Texas Train. Photo courtesy of the author.

Facing page

Top: With Chuck Conners, *Once Upon a Texas Train*. *Bottom:* A quiet
moment during the filming of *Once Upon a Texas Train*. Photos
courtesy of the author.

Above: On horseback, *Once Upon a Texas Train*. *Below:* A cameraman and I during shooting of *Once Upon a Texas Train*. Photos courtesy of the author.

Facing page

Top: Willie Nelson, Jack Elam and crew on the set of *Where the Hell's That Gold?*
Center: With Willie Nelson and Jack Elam on the set of *Where the Hell's That Gold?*
Bottom: Where the Hell's That Gold? Photos courtesy of the author.

Bottom and inset: Where the Hell's That Gold? Right: With Jack Elam on the set of *Where the Hell's That Gold?* Photos courtesy of the author.

David Huddleston and Chris Lloyd on the set of *Suburban Commando*. Photo courtesy of the author.

David Huddleston and I on the set of *Suburban Commando*. Photo courtesy of the author.

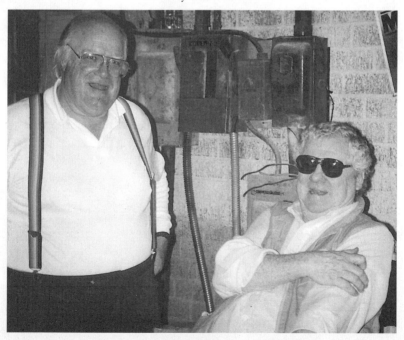

At Audie Murphy's grave in Arlington. Photo courtesy of the author.

Facing page

Top: David Huddleston, Ernie Borgnine and Denver Pyle at my
sixth annual seventieth birthday party. *Center:* Gene Evans, Jack Elam
and I in Ashland, Oregon. *Bottom:* My press meeting—standing in
for Clinton. Photos courtesy of the author.

Me and dog Gerti. Photo
courtesy of the author.

My Palm Springs star. Photo
courtesy of the author.

He said, "Fine, you can use the train. The only problem is we have a depot, but you can't get there from here. Where the tracks used to run across the highway has been paved over." There was no way to get the train from Ely to the depot.

We went out to look at the depot and it was perfect, but it was fifty miles from the train.

I said, "No problem. On the screen, I'll make it work." Which I did. If you've seen the picture, I have the train coming into the station. I took a baggage cart from outside the depot and put it in front of the camera at the train locations as a cutting piece and then brought the train in and stopped it. I took the cutting piece back to the depot fifty miles away and shot back over it. That way the train comes into the station and stops on the screen. On the screen, the train has pulled into the station, and actually, the station is fifty miles away from where the train actually was. It's a trick we use all the time.

I did it on a train in *Young Billy Young*. I brought the train right into the Old Tucson street. On the screen, you see it pull in, it stops, and the people get off and cross off camera. When they come from the street they get back on the train and the train pulls out. Actually, the train in that case was about a hundred and ten miles from the village where it stopped. And so those are the things you can do on the screen that we call "motion picture magic." Even a lot of people on the crews don't understand it, but it works. I've done it many times.

On *The Train Robbers* we built this little border village. We realized after it was built that we didn't have enough track coming into town. The figure to build more track was $80,000. I was there looking around with Michael Wayne and I said, "Well, why don't we just move the depot back another fifty yards, and that'll give us another fifty yards of track at the other end."

Everybody thought I was crazy, but we moved it back about fifty yards, and that in turn gave us about fifty yards at the other end of the track.

When we were working on *Where the Hell's That Gold?* we were using a train outside of Alamosa, Colorado. It was about a two-hour trip up to the location. We would go in trucks and meet the train, and the train would leave early in the morning. But on the way back, when we were through shooting for the day, we would get in the boxcars, and we would ride back in the train to the station in Alamosa.

I remember it was really the fun part of that picture, riding the train. Willie Nelson was with us, and Willie, Jack Elam, and I would play liar's poker all the way back to the station, which was about three hours, and we did that for about a week. That was fun. The picture wasn't.

*   *   *   *   *

On *The Good Guys and the Bad Guys* we had another two-hour run or so from the location up-track to Chama, where we were staying. Frankie Santillo was the editor. We put a cutting room on the train. We had our own generator, and we had our Moviolas. We were on the train for six weeks, so we had six weeks that we were able to cut while we were working.

I never had a train set—one of those Lionel electric trains that you used to get when you were a kid—but I got to play with my trains after I grew up. I'm always looking for a picture that has a train in it.

We ran off the track on that picture I was doing with Willie. A bunch of us were in the caboose and as we were pulling out of the station, we jumped the track. I don't know if you've ever been on a train that jumped the track, but you talk about an earthquake! The wheels that come off the one side are running on the ties, and it just about shook us to death.

We never really had any bad accidents, except for my blowing up and burning the bridge. That was kind of funny, because Red Adair, the famous oil-well firefighter, was called in to take a look at that bridge. The bridge cost about $250,000; it was all timbers. Usually Red Adair is called in to put out fires, but this fire was out by the time he got there, and he and his crew were put in charge of rebuilding the bridge.

When he heard it cost $250,000, Red Adair said, "No problem." It was in a wash, like a dry riverbed. He put about three huge galvanized steel pipes alongside of each other, then took bulldozers and pushed sand in between them and on top. It made the track level, and he and his men came up and laid more track across it. It cost around $18,000. We had to pay for it, so we were glad we didn't have to pay the two-fifty.

※　※　※　※　※

A Red Adair story. He said he went into a bar, and he sat down to have a drink, and a guy who was hard-of-hearing came up to him and said, "What's your name?"

He said, "Red Adair."

The guy said, "How did you like dancing with Ginger Rogers?"

※　※　※　※　※

Combat. Now, I've mentioned this before, about working with Vic Morrow. Even though I had made a feature-length picture and five other television shows before it, where I really learned physically how to make movies was when I was doing *Combat*. I did every other one with Robert Altman for about the first fifteen, and some of them were great.

The first episode I did was a show called "Far from the Brave" with Joe Mantell. You might remember Joe was the friend in *Marty* with Ernie Borgnine. "What're we gonna do tonight, Marty?" Marty would say, "I don't know, Angie." And Angie would say, "What're we gonna do tonight, Marty?" It was a running gag in the picture. Joe was a good actor.

The plot of the story was that a little cook's helper was sent up to take over the BAR, the Browning Automatic Rifle. There was one in each squad. The Browning man is killed at the beginning of the show, and the cook's helper takes over. There's a lot of jealousy between the boys.

There was a piece of action in the picture where Joe was caught in this group—the combat squad is in this town. The Germans come in with a panzer division. They've stayed there to be forward observers, and they get trapped in the town. In order to get out, they call a fire mission on themselves. As they're running out, I had three hundred explosions in one shot. It was the most effects men I have ever used on a show. There were twenty-three effects men in this one day working. This was for a television show in 1962!

In those days, an hour show cost about $130,000 to make. We used to do all sorts of wonderful big action scenes and explosions. Now they cost about a million.

In this one scene, Joe Mantell was supposed to dive for cover. Vic looks back and sees that he has his head in the ground, and he goes back and jumps in alongside of him. He plays a scene where he says, "You know, if you give up now, you're gonna give up the rest of your life." It was a good scene. Then there is a tremendous explosion and both of them are covered with rubble.

For this particular scene, they had drop-boards above the actors, which they'd tip over. Balsa wood, dirt, dust, and rubble would come pouring down on them. They seemed to overdo it this time, and there was this gigantic bunch of rubble that came crashing down on Vic and Joe. Once it cleared I cut the cameras and went in and started pulling all this debris aside, and when I got to Vic I said, "Vic, are you all right?"

He said, "Yeah, I'm okay."

I pulled him out, and even *deeper* in the rubble was poor Joe, and I had ignored him. Joe said, "What about me down here?" We pulled all of these timbers and stuff off him, and he said, "You don't care anything about me, you only care about the star!" I really felt bad about it. He wasn't hurt, just a little shook up. On Broadway he wasn't used to going around with any buildings falling on top of him.

In the final action, he was supposed to take his BAR gun and run across this bridge shooting Germans. The special effects crew had put these bullet hits in the rocks on this bridge, a string of small explosives that when touched off look like the actor is being shot at, and Joe asked me, "Now, are these gonna hurt me?"

I said, "No, they're fine."

What I didn't realize was that they had put the bullet hits in the night before, and the clay covering them had hardened, so when poor Joe came running up, and these bullet hits went off, they cut him right across the face. He went ahead and played his death scene with Vic, and when it was over he was actually cut up. I *really* felt bad about it. I think he was the only actor in all the time that I directed *Combat* who ever got hurt.

On that segment, where we had these three hundred explosions, I had a feeling that the only possible thing that could go wrong was that there were so many explosions and the dirt and dust could wipe out the shot. So I had them wire the explosions so we could rearm them right away, and go with a second take on it. This particular day, all the ABC head office guys from New York were out. They wanted to see us work, and so we had them up in like a little grandstand to watch this scene where we're blowing up the whole damn place.

We did it, and the guys were running through so much dust and dirt that you couldn't see anything. When it was over and everything settled down, and before anybody could complain about the fact that there was so much dirt, I said, "Let's go again."

All they had to do was rearm the bombs—it only took about three minutes—and we were ready to go again. Everybody thought I was kidding—how could they possibly go again? But in three minutes we did it again, and we did it with the right amount of dust, and this time it worked.

Some funny things happened on that show. Like for instance, one of the episodes I did was called "Walking Wounded." I thought it was going to be great. In the beginning of the show, Vic comes into this bombed-out French village and he goes into a women's garment store. While he's in there, he hears this dog whimpering. He looks under the table, and there's this little dog sitting there. Vic bends down and pets him. Then all of a sudden the Germans start firing at this town with heavy guns, and there's all these explosions. Vic gets under the table with the dog, and everything comes crashing down on him.

From then on, Vic and this dog are together for the rest of the show. They were supposed to be these great buddies. For instance, they were in a storm one night, and the dog is sitting out in the rain, and Vic takes his coat off and puts it around him— real tender things like that. The funny thing was, the dog didn't like Vic at all, and every time he got a chance, he'd bite him.

We'd be playing these real tender scenes, and the dog would reach up and nip Vic. Here we were playing the gentle side of this tough sergeant, and this great-looking dog just didn't like Vic at all. He didn't like sergeants, I guess, and every chance he got, he'd bite him. It was a riot. Talk about biting the hand that feeds you.

I wrote three originals for that show. I think one was called "Next in Command," with Ben Cooper, which was a good show, "Walking Wounded" is the one I talked about with Vic and the dog, and "Far from the Brave" was the first one. It was good, but then they started giving me scripts that other people had written.

Bob Altman was the senior member of the group, although actually, he wasn't there first. He came in and a pilot was made of *Combat.* It was the worst show that was ever made on *Combat.* It wasn't that it was so bad, it was just that I don't think anybody in the company, with the exception of the writer, Robert Pirosh, had done battleground. He knew something about war, but for some reason, everything was wrong. I mean, they weren't dressed right; they just didn't look like soldiers. It was not a good show. But the series was on for five years.

As these bad scripts would come in, Bob would turn them down and he'd give them to me. Then he'd take the good ones, or at least the ones that he had a chance to make good. He was, as was proven in later years, a very fine director. He's doing some wonderful work to this day, and he's a great guy. Very inventive; he would take a little idea from a script and would run with it, and make these very good shows.

I would end up doing the shows that had a lot of humor in them, and a lot of close connection with the boys in the squad. We really complimented each other, in that he would do a very good action show with a lot of characters, and I would do these shows with the boys so the audience got to know them.

Combat was a wonderful experience. I learned how to use the equipment and the actors were fine. We had some great actors on that show.

The first *Combat* was on television October 2, 1962, and the last telecast was August 29, 1967. Rick Jason played Lieutenant Hanley; Vic Morrow played Sergeant Sanders; Pierre Jalbert played Cage; Jack Hogan played Kirby; Dick Peabody played Lit-tlejohn; Tom Lowell played Private Billy Nelson; and Shecky Greene played Private Braddock.

Thanks to Leonard Maltin, I know all these wonderful things about the show.

I remember one time on *Combat* we were looking for locations. The Melody Ranch, which was the Gene Autry ranch out here in the San Fernando valley, had burned down about three weeks before we went out looking for locations, so I said, "Let's go look at it."

Everybody said, "It burned down."

I said, "Yeah, I know. Let's go look at it."

We went out there, and there was nothing left but chimneys and rubble. It worked perfectly. I used it in a show, and it worked as the place where the boys were stationed. It was supposed to be a bombed-out village. Actually it was a western town and it was fitting for me, being a western director, to do *Combat* in a western town, but nobody ever knew it.

Combat was also known for giving a lot of parts to stars, like Lee Marvin and Mickey Rooney. Mickey was in many of them. Just about every young actor in town played a part in *Combat* over the five years that it was on. It was very much like *Gunsmoke* on the western field. If you look at an old *Gunsmoke* you'll see people like Robert Redford just getting started.

I'm very thankful for having had the experience of doing *Combat*. After I'd done about six or seven episodes, I was asked to take over the whole show, but I said no, because if I was going to run the show, I wouldn't have time to do what I really knew how to do—write and direct. And they didn't really need me.

I was a little disappointed when it went from black and white to color, because we used to shoot our stuff in black and white, and people used to think that it was stock footage. What we did was we tried to make it grainy. Bob Hauser was a very good cameraman. People would swear that we had used stock footage, and we did on some occasions, where we had big explosions—bridges blowing up and such. But I would say that 99 percent of the film on *Combat* we shot ourselves.

It was a wonderful experience. I met some real great people. The producer of *Combat* was a fellow named Selig Seligman. Selig didn't really know anything about war or combat; his only connection with the war was that he was one of the prosecuting attorneys of the German war criminals at Nuremberg. That gave him some credentials.

A terrible tragedy occurred when Vic Morrow was killed in a helicopter accident in 1981. He was a very good friend of mine, and it was a terrible, terrible thing. I've never forgiven all those people who made that picture, *The Twilight Zone*, because somebody goofed, and it cost us a wonderful guy.

9

Getting Your Foot

in the Door

I love the line of Lewis Milestone. He directed *All Quiet on the Western Front, Of Mice and Men,* and many, many other great pictures. He was around town for years, and one time an interviewer asked him, "How does a director make out in Hollywood?" He responded, "Ask an alley cat." Milestone was absolutely right.

When you're a director and you finish a picture, it's like being an out-of-work astronaut. There are only so many rockets shot off in space every year, and you have to find some way to get on one. There's no book of rules. Everyone, whether they be an actor, a writer, or a director, has a different story about how he got his break in the picture business, and most of them are flukes—being in the right place at the right time.

I feel you have a much better shot at getting a break in the picture business if you are a writer, because nobody has to hire you. You can sit down and write. If you're an actor, a director, a cameraman, whatever, somebody has to give you a job. But a writer, if he gets a good idea, can sit down and write it. Then, if it's good enough, somebody reads it and wants to do it, and he's off and running.

Charlton Heston tells a story about working over at Paramount. He was leaving the studio one day and he had the top down on his convertible. Cecil B. DeMille and his assistant were walking by the car, and for no reason at all, Heston waved to him, then kept going. DeMille said to his assistant, "Who's that?"

The assistant knew Charlton Heston, and he told DeMille who he was. DeMille said, "I want to test him for *The Ten Commandments*." Heston got the job. He later said, "If I'd've had the top up on that convertible, I would have never had the break that launched my career."

Alan Ladd was an extra and some executive noticed him in the crowd, and the rest is history.

Randolph Scott was a semipro golfer. He was up in Pebble Beach playing in a tournament, and a producer noticed him. He hired him to play a naval officer in a picture, and his career was launched.

Marion Davies took a shine to Joel McCrea when he was doing a bit in a picture at Paramount. She went to her friend William Randolph Hearst and insisted that they use Joel in her next picture, which they did. Joel was around making pictures for the next fifty years.

Then there are those who never get a break. But I've always said, "Hollywood is like a poker game. You have to stay in till you get a good hand."

❖   ❖   ❖   ❖   ❖

There are things in the picture business that really strike me funny. For instance, I was in London getting ready to do *Hannie Caulder* and the production manager wanted me to meet a British cameraman. The reason he wanted a British cameraman is because they worked cheaper than American cameramen. If he could get me to accept this cameraman, he could save a lot of money.

It was arranged that I would meet the production manager and Ted Skaife, an excellent cameraman who worked many times for David Lean. We were to meet at the Inn on the Park, which is one of a number of high-class hotels along the parkway in London.

We were to have tea one afternoon, and we arrived at the dining room. I was introduced to Ted Skaife, a really fine English gentleman. He was reading a copy of the *London Times*. We sat down and had tea, and it was very pleasant. The production manager was bending over backward to make a go of it between us, to make sure that we liked each other, so that he could hire him.

A postscript on this is that the production manager had made a deal with the production company that if he brought the picture in under budget, he would get a $10,000 bonus. Now, the production people always talked to the wrong people. They always talked to the cameraman or the production manager. They should always talk to the director. Not that I ever made any kind of a deal like that, but I always resented when somebody did, and I found out about it. But that had nothing to do with the cameraman Ted Skaife, really, because he was a top-notch cameraman, and I liked him. Ted got the job.

It was a very, very pleasant day in London. And now, we dissolve, and we're six weeks into the picture. One day Ted Skaife looked out and saw the production manager putting a number of lights into a truck. We were in Almería, and the truck was heading back to Madrid. So Ted Skaife collared this production manager, and he started calling him every name in the book. Then he came to me, and he said, "Do you know what this sonofabitch is doing?! He's taking lights away from me."

I started to laugh, because I remembered this wonderful tea we'd had, where everyone was so cordial to each other, and now, when the chips were down, out in the field, and the production manager was trying to cut corners, the you-know-what hit the fan. And it always does. I've seen it happen time and time again.

Very few production managers know how to spend money to save money. As a rule, they'll save you money even if it costs you every dime you've got.

10

Actors and

Others

Lee J. Cobb was probably one of the finest actors to come from Broadway. He came out to Hollywood and made many, many pictures. I met him and worked with him on a show. I'd been hired by Universal to do the first ninety-minute television show that had ever been made. They gave me the Owen Wister novel *The Virginian* and a set of characters. They said, "Do a script," which I did. It was to be the first *Virginian,* which turned out to be a long-running series. But actually, it wasn't the first one made. There was another one they decided to make first, and then I made the second one, with Lee J. Cobb as the head of the ranch.

This is kind of a horror story, because I had so looked forward to working with him. I went out and I found the locations, and we prepared the show. The day before the show, I got laryngitis, and I couldn't say a word. So here we go, up in the pines on Mount Pinus. It was a big day, with cattle stampedes and some heavy scenes between Lee J. and the boys who played Trampas and the Virginian, and so on, and I couldn't talk. I couldn't say a word.

Lee J. thought, What a great director, he doesn't talk. I *couldn't* talk. I could make little sounds, so the assistant sort of knew what I wanted to do, but it was absolute terror for the first two days. I got well, and then I got to know Lee J., who had a great sense of humor.

I would take him to lunch, and in those days I had a little white Mazda. I wish I still had it. Lee J. told me so many wonderful stories, one of which I've never forgotten.

When *Death of a Salesman* opened on Broadway, it was a complete smash. It had been playing for about six months, and Lee J. said, "As you do, even though it was a dynamite play, the actors got lazy." So this one Saturday, they had done a matinee. When they finished the evening show, the director, who had been in the audience, and Arthur Miller, the playwright, came backstage, and the director chewed the cast out, saying, "You're getting lazy. You're not hitting this play like you should." He really gave it to them.

The topper was, he said, "We're going to do a rehearsal." Now, they had done the show twice that day, and Lee recalled, "We were exhausted, but he made us go out to an empty theater and do a full rehearsal of the show. I've never forgotten it. So when I do a show where I'm working very hard, I make sure that I'm working on all cylinders all the time, because the director and the author are liable to be out there in the audience and come back and make me do it again."

He was a great guy, and as I say, he had a wonderful sense of humor. I remember we were talking about the script, and he was making certain suggestions. When we got in my car and were driving back to the set, he said, "This car is awful loud—I rewrite mufflers, too." He was a darling guy, and I was so sad to hear that he'd died. I knew he had a bad heart. As a matter of fact, when we were working, those first couple of days up in the mountains, there was some concern about him. The heart finally caught up to him. He was a great actor, and it was a great privilege for me to have been around him.

✿   ✿   ✿   ✿   ✿

Robert Ryan was another excellent actor, and he was in the first picture I directed, a terrible thing called *The Canadians*.

When the picture was over, we flew from somewhere in Canada to Vancouver, and we were waiting for a plane to take us down to Los Angeles. It was about two o'clock in the morning. There was a reporter there who had been waiting for some government dignitary who hadn't shown up. Here this reporter was in the middle of the night, so he came over to us.

He said to Bob Ryan, "Mr. Cameron, could we do an interview for radio?"

Bob looked at him and said, "Fine. But you have to interview my friend Frank Gruber here."

Now, Frank Gruber was a writer in Hollywood. I went along with the joke, and the reporter interviewed Robert Ryan as Rod Cameron. He asked him about all the pictures, all the westerns he'd done, and Bob went right along with it. Luckily, he knew quite a bit about Rod Cameron, and I knew Frank Gruber, because I'd done a rewrite on one of his scripts once. The whole interview was conducted with Rod Cameron and Frank Gruber . . . who were actually Robert Ryan and Burt Kennedy.

The plane finally came, and we got on. We were flying United and had to change planes in San Francisco for some reason. Bob and I were sitting together, and just before we landed in San Francisco, the stewardess came up and said, "Mr. Kennedy, I'm sorry, but this seat has been sold from San Francisco down to L.A., and you're going to have to get off this plane and catch another."

I was mad, but there was nothing I could do about it, so when we landed in San Francisco I got off the plane and waited around for about two hours to catch another plane going down to L.A. The next day I ran into Bob Ryan, and I told him how mad I was that I'd been thrown off the plane. He said, "You'd be madder yet if you knew that no one got on the plane. I sat all alone on the way back."

✻　✻　✻　✻　✻

One of the worst plane rides I ever had was coming back from San Antonio, Texas. Actually, we were coming from Brackettville, Texas, where they had built the set for *The Alamo*. We got into one of those horrendous thunderstorms coming out of San Antonio. I was sitting with Richard Widmark, who hates to fly—he's a white-knuckler. I guess he had an ulcer besides, because he drank milk while we were bouncing around in the sky. John Wayne was sitting up front playing poker with some guys, and he wasn't paying any attention to it. I'd look down the aisle while we were bouncing around, and the plane was corkscrewing.

Then there was this loud bang as the plane was struck by lightning, and so help me, I saw this blue whatever-it-was come right down the aisle, heading toward the back of the plane. There was an explosion, and then everything was fine. I was told later that we'd been struck by lightning. What happens is that when it hits the plane, because the plane isn't grounded, it eventually jumps off the plane into the clouds, and when it does, it burns a hole in the tail of the plane. It was pretty hairy.

Well, Richard Widmark is one of my favorite people in the picture business. Unfortunately, I didn't get to work with him until late in his career, when we worked on *The Alamo* together. He would come over to my house when I lived over in Royal Oaks and we would rehearse, and actually do a little rewrite on his part. He was excellent in that picture.

Another fellow in that picture who was a dear friend of mine was Denver Pyle. Chill Wills was also a dear friend, and a really fine actor. As he said, he put a lot of "jelly roll" in his parts. He was nominated for an Academy Award for his role in *The Alamo*. He took out an ad in the trade papers that everybody got up in arms about. I think it said something like, "The men at the Alamo would have been pulling for me to win the Oscar." Everybody was upset about it. I don't know why, but they thought it was in bad taste.

Chill called his wife "The Ramrod." Apparently she made wonderful chili, and he was always saying, "You gotta come up to the house and have chili." One day, after about twenty-five years, I did. I got so sick, I couldn't walk the next day. I never told Chill.

Another actor in *The Alamo,* who played Colonel Travis, was Laurence Harvey, whom I had met years before at Warner Bros. I did a script for him, as a matter of fact, called *A Distant Trumpet.* There were big plans for it; it was going to be directed by Jack Clayton and star Harvey, Jack Hawkins, and Alec Guinness. As it turned out, it was made as a very cheap picture. Raoul Walsh directed it, and to me, it was a big disappointment, because the original book by Paul Horgan was dynamite.

Remembering *The Alamo,* Richard Boone was a dear friend. He played Sam Houston. Pat Wayne, of course, played Bonham, and he was and still is a dear friend. Ken Curtis, who played Captain Dickinson, was also a close friend. Carlos Aruza, the sensational bullfighter who was killed about twenty years ago in a car accident, played one of Santa Anna's messengers. Then there were Guinn "Big Boy" Williams, Chuck Roberson, Hank Worden, and Olive Carey (Harry Carey's widow, and mother of Harry Carey Jr.) It was quite a cast.

It was Duke's dream to make that picture, and he tried for many years to get it made. Of course, when it was made, United Artists said it cost more than it actually did, and said it lost money, which is not true. It even made a little.

A funny thing happened on that picture, right about in the middle of it. John Ford showed up on the set down in Brackettville, unannounced. He hadn't told anybody; he just showed up, got in the director's chair, and sat down right next to the camera.

Duke went to Bill Clothier, the cameraman, and said, "Bill, what am I gonna do? I can't ask him to leave, but I can't have him here, because everybody's gonna say that he directed the picture."

Bill said, "Well, I've got an extra camera crew here for the second unit. Why don't we just send him out and do some shots—you know, cavalry crossing the river, horses, all that stuff."

So Duke said, "Great," and made Michael Wayne the assistant. Duke kept telling him, "Don't let him talk to any of the actors."

Michael and John Ford went off with a bunch of cavalry guys and wagons, and they shot for four or five days. Ford got bored, packed up, and left. He wasn't mad or anything, he just thought he'd helped as much as he could. Duke was really glad to see him go.

Being a director, I know it's really tough when people try to take over, or try to tell you what to do. I did *Big Bad John* down in Texas, and the first day, I was doing a scene with Jack Elam and Ned Beatty. There was a dog in the scene, and the dog trainer was a pain in the ass.

He kept saying, "Look, the scene is better if Jack comes from over here, because that way the dog can see me," and all this baloney.

I took it as long as I could, and finally I said, "Look, get a car, put the trainer in it, put the dog in it, and get 'em the hell out of here!" It shook everybody up, but I couldn't have a dog trainer directing the picture.

It was funny, after I did that the prop man made me a suggestion box—which didn't have a hole in it for you to drop your suggestions. I've still got it.

I try not to throw my weight around on a set, and I don't expect anybody else, cast or crew, to either. When they do, I get a little nasty. Maybe it's old age. I have a saying: "There's a fine line between mellowing and not giving a shit."

✿   ✿   ✿   ✿   ✿

I seldom, if ever, have had any problems with temperament on a set, mostly because I kind of try to create, like John Huston said he used to do, an atmosphere where everyone can do his best work and not be afraid of somebody coming down on them. When you do that, you usually have a happy set. Now, you can go too far the other way. Once in a while, if you're too loose and easygoing, people have a tendency to try to take advantage of you, and then you have to put your foot down and really go after 'em.

I learned from John Wayne and Yul Brynner about yelling at people on the set. They said, "Never do it when you're mad, because when you're mad, you forget what you want to say. So just pick your time, when you're very calm, and then let 'em have it." I learned well the technique of chewing people out from John Wayne. And when I get mad, really mad, the leaves fall off the trees. It works. Luckily, I've seldom had to do that. But once in a while, you really have to be the bad guy.

You always risk the crew's going around after that saying, "Gee, I thought he was such a nice guy, I didn't realize he was such a jerk," but you have to do it. I equate the picture business very much with the Army. In the Army, you have your generals, and you have a captain, and you have sergeants, and then you have the enlisted men. You have to keep your position, as if you were in a war.

It would be as if in the middle of a big battle a private went up to the general and said, "General, don't you think it would be better if you had the cavalry attack after the artillery?" They'd put him up against the wall and shoot him.

Well, it's the same way with the picture business. You can't have the privates telling the majors what to do. It's exactly the same. In the Army, they call it "chain of command." And in the picture business, if you keep your chain of command intact, it works. One thing that is different from the Army is that the director is the first among equals. He has to run the show—and if he *doesn't* run the show, you have complete chaos. Another lesson.

❀   ❀   ❀   ❀   ❀

Ricardo Montalban had been working at MGM for many years in pictures with the swimmer Esther Williams. He'd never done anything with any real heavyweight directors at Metro, and there were a number of them there at the time, including Mervyn LeRoy.

He finally got a picture with Lana Turner that Mervyn was going to direct. The day came for his first big scene, Ricardo couldn't wait, because Mervyn was a great director and was going to give him really special directions on how to do this scene with Lana.

The actor went out on the set, and Mervyn put Lana at one end of a sofa, and Ricardo at the other end, and said, "Rehearse."

They rehearsed this two- or three-page scene, and LeRoy didn't say a word. When they were through, he said, "All right, well, let's make it."

Ricardo was thinking, This is a great director? The soundman said "Speed . . . rolling," or however they do that; I've forgotten—I've only made seventy-five pictures. Anyway, he said "Roll 'em, speed," and Mervyn started to say "Action," but somebody started hammering, and Mervyn yelled, "Hold it! Hold it!" He turned around and announced to the stage, "Pay a little respect to these actors—just hold the work!"

He turned back, and they said, "Roll 'em, speed," and before Mervyn said "Action," he turned back and said, "You know, we don't make noise when *you* people are working. We don't bother you, and we expect the same respect from you! We're trying to do a scene here!"

He turned back again, and Ricardo was all set to go, and they said, "Roll 'em, speed," and Mervyn turned around again and said, "As a matter of fact, if you don't hold the work, you're gonna be very sorry! I've been in the picture business for twenty-five years, and I just won't stand for this!"

Mervyn kept this up, and kept it up, and kept going back to start the scene, and just as he'd go to start it, he'd think of something else to say, and he'd turn around and scream again. Ricardo said this went on for about twenty minutes, until finally the director said okay, and they said "Roll 'em, speed," and Mervyn clapped his hands and said, "Now—a lot of energy, guys! Action!"

Ricardo said that was it. "I expected something magic to happen, but he never said a word. That was my first experience with a top director at Metro-Goldwyn-Mayer."

And LeRoy *was* a top director. He had made pictures like *Quo Vadis, No Time for Sergeants, The Bad Seed, Waterloo Bridge, Random Harvest, Little Caesar,* and *I am a Fugitive from a Chain Gang.* Big pictures. Little talent—big pictures.

Mervyn had married Jack Warner's daughter. Not a bad idea.

✩   ✩   ✩   ✩   ✩

The actor I've probably known longer than anyone else in Hollywood is Denver Pyle. People know him as Uncle Jesse on *The Dukes of Hazzard*, but he's done other things that were very good.

I knew Denver back in the forties when he was a struggling actor. The first interview he went on was for a submarine picture. They needed a commander on a German submarine, so Denver put on a black turtleneck and a Navy pea coat so that he looked like a sailor and went over to interview for the part. He thought it would be impressive if he said he was German and pretended he couldn't speak English.

They brought him in, and he had learned to say in German that he didn't speak English, and that's what he did. They were very impressed, but he didn't get the part.

He was always doing things like that. For instance, he went to a spot in Los Angeles called the Adventurer's Club. It's similar to the Savage Club in London. Denver had been invited by some members he had met because he had told them about a cruise he'd taken around the world on a sailboat. It wasn't true, but it sounded good.

He went to a meeting where there were a group of true adventurers, people who had been around the world in boats and climbed the Himalayas. They were now in their eighties and nineties and used crutches, canes, and wheelchairs.

Denver stood up in front of these hundred or so men and started telling a story about how he had sailed to an uncharted island in the South Pacific. He told them there was a lagoon on the island, with a cliff that came down on both sides, forming a V right down into the water. Once a year, the sun set exactly in the middle of this V and the natives had a big celebration. Hundreds of them supposedly did an intricate dance to the island drums, all of them holding pieces of rope or vine. When they finished this dance, he continued, they made a giant fishnet out of this rope and vine, all the while circling over and under, up and down, and jumping. He went on to explain that they then used this net to catch fish for the island for the whole year, by the end of which it was practically worn out.

Denver got about three-quarters of the way through the story and looked out at these guys, thinking they were looking at him strangely because he was in the middle of telling a gigantic lie. He finally finished the story by saying that one day he was going to sail off in another boat and return to the island. He told them he could locate it by his charts and that his dream was to return there and see the natives dance again.

When he finished there was complete silence. He looked out, and to him they all looked like they were going to storm the podium and kill this fraud. Then, all of a sudden, one of the adventurers started pounding his cane on the floor. One by one, the other members picked up the rhythm; it was like applause. Finally, one of them stood up and said, "Mr. Pyle, that is the greatest adventure we have ever heard, and we thank you for coming to the Adventurer's Club and sharing it with us." Denver was relieved, to say the least.

He was always pulling his stunts. I remember one time we were invited to what they called in the early days a "bottle party," to which you'd bring your own bottle.

I arrived at the door of the party house at the same time Denver did. Now, Denver was broke, as we all were, and he didn't bring a bottle. I was carrying a brown bag with the smallest bottle of gin you could buy, the kind you could slip in your back pocket like a flask, and a bottle of tonic water.

Denver said, "Let me carry that in for you, Burt." I gave him the bag and we went in together, and he was the one carrying the bag of booze. The hostess met him at the door and pulled out this bottle of gin. Denver looked at me and said, "I've never been so embarrassed in my life." He hadn't brought anything, but he made it look like *I* hadn't and that *he* was the embarrassed party!

Last year, at my Fourth Annual Seventieth Birthday Party, Denver walked in with a paper bag. In it was a tiny bottle of cheap gin. It is still on the shelf in my bar.

Denver got me involved in another situation. He had a friend named Hallier DuBarrier. DuBarrier was a world adventurer who had once been a general in the Chinese Air Force and fought for Chiang Kai-shek. With all his adventures he was a great storyteller, so all the wealthy people in upstate New York would invite him to their estates, where he would entertain them with his colorful tales.

He was invited to the Mellon family estate in Connecticut, and while roaming the grounds he found an old chicken coop way out in back, in terrible disrepair. He got an idea, and made a sign that read, THE ROCK RIFT POLO CLUB, which he nailed above the door of the chicken coop.

He then went to a very exclusive printing shop and had beautiful, gold-trimmed invitations made up—invitations to become a nonriding member of "The Rock Rift Polo Club," for which he included the address. He sent them to Churchill, to Eisenhower, to heads of state all over the world. A number of them signed up and sent back the applications and became nonriding members of "The Rock Rift Polo Club," which was nothing more than a chicken coop.

Knowing about this, Denver came to me with an application. He said, "Here's an opportunity to join a polo club in Connecticut. I'm not at all sure they will accept you, but fill out the application and send it in. I'm already a member."

I filled out the application and I got a membership card as a nonriding member of "The Rock Rift Polo Club" signed by General Hallier DuBarrier, along with a list of names of everyone else who had joined. It was amazing how many had fallen for the gag. Little did they know they belonged to a chicken coop.

Years later, when I joined "The Hollywood Turf Club," Mervyn LeRoy was its president. On the application, it asked what clubs I belonged to. I filled in "The Players" in New York, of which I was a member, and "The Rock Rift Polo Club" of Connecticut. My application went through without any trouble.

When Denver decided to direct pictures, he got a deal to do a couple of episodes of *Death Valley Days*. Ronald Reagan was the host of these stories about the twenty-mule teams in California.

They went up to the sand dunes outside of Lone Pine. They were doing this story about an old prospector, played by Strother Martin. Strother had this pack mule, and the scene called for him to come down this sandy hill toward the camera, leading the mule.

It was really hot, as it usually is up in Lone Pine, and Denver said, "Now Strother, you take the mule, circle around so you don't make tracks in the sand, and come up that slope. When you get just about in sight of the camera, I'll yell action, and you come on over the crest leading this mule, and come on down past the camera. That's the shot."

So Strother said, "Okay." He took the mule, and he made a wide circle around. Denver gave him enough time to make it up the other side of the hill and to be ready to come over the crest, and then yelled, "Action!" Nothing happened.

So again Denver yelled, "Action! Strother, come on! Action!" They waited and waited; no Strother, and no mule. Finally Denver got real mad, and yelled, "Goddamnit, Strother, bring that mule over the hill!"

Finally Strother appeared at the top of the hill, and he yelled down, "The mule fainted!"

What had happened was that this mule was packed with all this mining equipment, and when Strother had tried to turn him around to come up the hill, the mule fell over. And he was lying in the sand, and he couldn't get up because he had this pack strapped on him. And Strother was yelling, "We've gotta do something! He fainted! He passed out! It's too hot to work."

Well, the crew managed to get the mule back up on his feet, and they went back down the hill, but now they'd made all these tracks in the sand in front of the camera, so Denver had to go find another hill.

They got set up, and Denver gave Strother the same instructions, and they waited and waited, and when they thought he'd had time to get to the crest of the hill, Denver yelled, "Action!"

Here came Strother once more, and he yelled, "He fainted *again*!"

I don't know if they ever got the shot.

*   *   *   *   *

Strother Martin was a wonderful character. For those of you who don't recognize the name, he was in *Cool Hand Luke,* and *Butch Cassidy and the Sundance Kid,* among other films. I had him in

Hannie Caulder. He was in many, many pictures, and was a big favorite of Sam Peckinpah's. I don't think Sam ever made a picture without him. He was a complete delight.

He was married to a woman named Helen, and she was as much of a character as Strother was. I remember when we were in Spain making *Hannie Caulder,* she was the efficiency expert. I mean, she would sit and eat dinner with you, and when the check would come, she'd go over it item by item. She would take twenty minutes, and call the headwaiter over and question certain things, like the cost of certain items—she was wonderful. She'd do the same thing on the hotel bills, not only theirs, but everybody else's. She just wanted to make sure that no one got cheated.

If you were having a party, you never had to worry about entertainment. All you had to do was invite Strother and Helen—they were fabulous.

A footnote to Strother's wife: When *Hannie Caulder* finished, the company that financed it ran out of money. Matter of fact, they tried to get me to take the negative back to London in my luggage, and I refused to do it. There was some money that hadn't been paid to the actors, and who do you suppose went in and faced down the powers that be at this London company? Helen, and she got all the money for all the actors. I don't think anyone ever knew that.

✧   ✧   ✧   ✧   ✧

One of my favorite people in the picture business is Tony Randall. Tony is a very accomplished actor, and calls himself the "King of Comedy." He made the mistake of saying that in front of Harry Morgan, who disagreed with him.

We did a show together and he was charming. He does have a personality. If you're going to be around Tony Randall, you must remember he knows everything, and act accordingly.

I once worked with Rod Steiger on a picture, and he told me a story about when he was doing *On the Waterfront* with Marlon Brando. They did that famous scene in the backseat of the car where Brando was blaming his brother, played by Steiger, for not doing right by him. It was the scene where he's saying, "I could have been a contender."

Steiger said that they did the scene in a two-shot. They did a close-up of Brando and when it came time for Steiger's close-up, Brando went home. The script supervisor had to read Brando's lines. I was telling this to Tony Randall, and he said, "That didn't happen."

I retorted, "Well, Steiger said it did."

"Well, it couldn't have happened."

I asked why. He said, "Because there were no close-ups in the backseat in that scene."

I felt ridiculous, because here I'd made such a point of the story and Tony was so sure that it was all done in a two-shot that I backed down and said, "Well, all right." I ran the picture again, and he was completely wrong. There were close-ups, but that is the way Tony is. He attacks so well. As I say, he is charming. I loved working with him and I love seeing him interviewed. He's brilliant, and I understand he has a theater in New York that he runs with his money. I know he's an opera freak; he knows every one.

We did a scene in a picture where he was in his office in a big ranch house. One of the prop people had put a harp in his office. We got ready to do the scene with Burgess Meredith. Burgess comes in and plays this scene with him, and I said, "Tony, why don't you play the scene practicing on your harp?" He practiced his harp all the way through the scene. He wasn't afraid to try anything. I really love him as an actor and would have liked to have done more with him.

He was interviewed not long ago on television, discussing a Broadway play of his—a flop. He didn't say it was a failure. He said, "There's not a day goes by that nobody talks about it."

Another favorite of mine in Hollywood was a punch-drunk fighter named Ralph Volke. He fought in the late thirties and early forties, some pretty big boxers. He ended up working the corner of many big fighters. Any fight picture from the thirties, you'll see Ralph in the corner, working as a cut man, or whatever.

As I say, he was punch-drunk, but a nice guy. When I knew him, he was John Wayne's personal masseur. He used to give Duke rubdowns before a picture would start to get Duke in shape. He would go along wherever we went on location. His job was to give Duke a rubdown whenever he wanted it.

Ralph was a talker. You couldn't understand what he was saying, but he would talk all the time. He was always complaining that he was having a heart attack and how bad it was. But he was always there. We would give him a line whenever we could so he could make some money. I had him in *The War Wagon* and I think everything I ever did with Duke we found a place for Ralph.

He lived in a hotel in Hollywood, just off Hollywood and Vine, and you would always see him hanging out down there in the street. Between pictures, he was always broke. He came to me and he wanted me to loan him some money, I gave it to him and as soon as he went to work, he paid me back. With that loan, I bought a friend for life—a friend such as you seldom find in this town.

For instance, he was on a picture and he was shooting the bull one night with a makeup guy; I won't mention his name, since he was a real jerk. My name came up because I had been with Wayne for so many years.

This makeup guy said, "Oh, Kennedy can't direct traffic." Ralph decked him. He hit him with a right hand and knocked the guy on his ass. He stood over him and said, "Burt Kennedy is a friend of mine and you can't talk like that about him." I don't know of anyone else in this town who would have stood up for me like that. Not my agent, that's for sure.

Ralph is gone now, but I will never forget him.

* * * * *

I did a promo for a series of two-hour *Bonanza* episodes up in Lake Tahoe. David Dortort was the producer. He had been the producer of the long-running series for twenty years or so.

Years earlier, I'd seen a show David Dortort wrote for *Zane Grey Theater*. This is back almost forty years ago, and it was very good. I was working at Warners at the time, and I wrote him a fan letter. He wrote back thanking me. Now you dissolve, and it's forty years later. Warners asked me to be the producer and director of a show, which I agreed to, and then they asked me to be the executive producer of another pilot that was being directed by Bob Totten. I had nothing to do with it, really, but they wanted me to be the executive producer, which I was.

They made the pilot and sent it to New York. Somebody called me and said, "I've got bad news. The pilot did not sell." It was a show called *The Cowboys* that was taken from the John Wayne picture about these young kids who take a herd of cattle cross-country.

About an hour later, they called me back and said, "We have good news and bad news. The good news is that we sold the series. The bad news is that it will be on a network where you are doing another show, CBS. They figure that producing both shows would be a conflict of interest. Can you suggest somebody to produce the show?"

I suggested David Dortort. They thought that was a wonderful idea. Then they called me back in another hour and said, "David is willing to produce *The Cowboys* as long as you don't have anything to do with it."

I had a contract that paid me for every show made, whether I did it or not, so I didn't really care. But I thought it was strange that the guy I'd recommended for the job had shot me down.

Now we dissolve again, and I'm doing this promo for David Dortort. One day I saw him and I told him this story about what happened. He denied it completely. He said, "Oh, that never happened. I would never do such a thing." I'm sure he did.

When I finished the promo, which turned out quite well, I was coming down the elevator with David. We were heading for the airport to go home, and he said to me, "You know, it's amazing that all these years we've both been doing westerns, we never worked together. Of course, I have heard that you are difficult, but you've probably heard the same thing about me."

I said, "David, I never heard of you at all." As you might guess, I didn't do the shows when they were finally sold to NBC.

✧   ✧   ✧   ✧   ✧

Pat Buttram, Gene Autry's comic sidekick, loved telling stories about Gene. They weren't too flattering, which is what made them funny. He said that right after World War II, they were entertaining in an Army hospital in a ward for wounded soldiers who were recuperating. Pat told a couple of jokes and then Gene played his guitar and sang a few songs.

When he finished his last song, he saw a soldier sitting on his bunk, staring at the wall in silence. Gene walked down to his bunk and played and sang a song just for this boy. When he finished, the boy just kept staring at the wall. Gene put his arm around him and said, "I hope you get better, son." The kid replied, "I hope you do, too."

During their drinking days, Pat was pretty close to being a drunk. They were to meet at the bar at the Brown Derby on Vine Street. Gene walked in and looked around and didn't see Pat. He walked up to the bar and said to the bartender, "I'm supposed to meet Pat Buttram here. Have you seen him?" The bartender said, "You're standing on him."

Gene has owned the California Angels for many years and they have never been able to win the pennant. Pat said, "Waiting for the California Angels to win a pennant is like leaving the landing lights on for Amelia Earhart."

When people accused Pat Buttram of drinking too much, he used to say, "I only drink to have something to do when I'm drunk."

✵   ✵   ✵   ✵   ✵

Robert Mitchum is very professional and one of the finest actors I have worked with. I did two pictures in a row with him. He's amazing in that if you listen to him you think he's a little crazy, but he's not at all. He is one of the brightest guys I know.

He tells a great story about John Huston. They were doing *Heaven Knows, Mr. Allison,* and they were in the last three or four days of the picture when Huston just disappeared. As it turned out, he was managing a boxer who had a fight somewhere and he wanted to be there for it. It was a Fox picture, and everybody panicked. The studio sent all of these executives to the location. Somebody asked Mitch, "Where's John Huston?"

Mitch said, "He left."

"He just left?"

Mitch shrugged and said, "You know how he hates good-byes."

The first time I met Mitchum was in Spain. I had gone over there with Max Youngstein, who used to be the head of United Artists, and was then an independent producer. Actually, he was over there to see Bob and I was over there to see Yul Brynner. They were making a picture called *Villa Rides*. Charlie Bronson was in the picture, I believe, playing a Mexican.

We went to Madrid, went out on the set, and sat down. I started talking to Mitchum and I really liked him. Brynner said. "We're going to have a party tonight. I'll come to your suite"—we were staying at the Castellana Hilton—"and we'll have a party."

That night, Mitchum, who was staying at the same hotel, came to the room; Max Youngstein was there and a marvelous guy named Jim Hennigan, who had been a publicity man for Wayne. We had drinks and hors d'oeuvres and sat around drinking and shooting the bull. It got to be four o'clock in the morning and Mitch finally said, "I don't think Brynner's going to throw a party." He left. Brynner never did show up.

Speaking of Jim Hennigan, I remember when he worked for John Wayne. He was the only one who stood up to Duke. One day he stood up once too often and he was out. That's how he ended up in Spain as an expatriate.

He was a classic press man. All the Hollywood expatriates in Madrid, including actor Lawrence Tierney and director Nicholas Ray, lived in nice apartments on a street named Doctor Fleming. I went over to Jimmy's apartment one night in the rain. When it was time to leave, I said, "Well, I'll go down and catch a cab."

Jim questioned me. "A cab?" He went on, "You're the director of a big motion picture and you are not going home in a cab. Who's the production manager on your picture?" I told him, "Bob Goodstein."

He called the hotel and got Bob on the phone and said, "Bob, the director of your picture is over here, and he doesn't have a car and driver. That's an insult. If you don't send the car and driver over here to such-and-such Doctor Fleming in twenty minutes, I'm going to call an ambulance. I will send him back to the hotel in an ambulance with red lights and sirens, so it's up to you." Within twenty minutes, there was a car and driver at the front door.

Jim had a way about him. I guess he learned a lot from being around Duke, because he was very good. He wrote a column for years for *The Hollywood Reporter*, similar to the one Army Archerd writes for *Variety*. While he was working there, he bought a new Cadillac, fancy clothes, watches, and so on. The editor of *The Hollywood Reporter* came to him and asked, "Jimmy, how can you afford all these wonderful things? I mean, I'm only paying you seven hundred a week to write this column." Jimmy said, "I'm selling space in my column for a thousand dollars a line. When a press guy calls me and wants me to plug something in the column, I sell it to him."

Jim actually promoted the last two million dollars for John Wayne's *The Alamo*. I was there when he did it. We were staying at Fort Clark in Brackettville, Texas, and he got on the phone to some money people in Texas. He closed the deal and enabled Duke to start *The Alamo*. Then Jimmy claimed Duke reneged on the deal he had made and they had a big spat. They didn't talk to each other again for years.

Both of them wanted to talk. They would speak to me and Jimmy would say, "Tell Duke . . ." and Duke would say, "Tell Jimmy . . ." This went on for years. It was much like the other Jimmy, writer James Edward Grant, who had a split-up with Duke. They got back together again on *Circus World* in Spain. Frank Capra was directing it, but Duke fired him—*fired* Frank Capra!—and brought in Henry Hathaway. Then he brought in Jimmy Grant to do a rewrite on the script.

Jimmy didn't like Henry Hathaway, and he wouldn't talk to him. They would meet in Duke's room while they were working on the script, and Jimmy would say to Duke, "You tell Hathaway . . ." Henry was right there in the room, but Jimmy wouldn't talk to him directly. Hathaway would in turn ask Duke to talk to Jimmy. They were like little kids. Somehow they did manage to make the picture, and it was pretty good.

Getting back to Mitchum, John Wayne's company was preparing for a picture called *Blood Alley* and they wanted Mitch for the lead in the part of a skipper of a steamboat on the Yangtze River in China. It was a decent picture which Bill Wellman ended up directing.

Later, during preparation, they went up to San Rafael in California to a place called China Camp and built a set. They bought a steamboat that this Mitchum character was to skipper, and they started the picture. George Coleman was Duke's transportation captain, and was a pain in the ass.

About a week or two into the picture, Mitch got mad at Coleman for some reason and threw him into the river. He then proceeded to go into the production office and throw a tantrum. He broke up the place. William Wellman got on the phone to Duke in Hollywood and said, "Duke, we've got to replace Mitchum— he's impossible."

Duke asked, "With who?"

Wellman said, "With you."

And they did.

The same thing happened with Wellman on *The High and the Mighty*. Spencer Tracy was to play the part of the pilot, but for some reason he couldn't, so Duke took over.

Ernest Borgnine! Jack Elam calls him Ernie Bombastic. He said Ernie would never let him sleep in when they were rooming next to each other during the filming of *Hannie Caulder*. Early every morning, Ernie would proclaim, "Oh, what a beautiful morning," or "It's a beautiful day."

Ernie's beautiful wife Tova sells products that make people look young. Ernie, on the other hand, keeps everyone young.

He is an absolute tonic to be around. He has more energy than a truckload of Jack LaLannes, and a sweeter man never walked the earth.

Ernie is eighty, a fact Jack Elam is constantly reminding him of. But he goes through life like a runaway train! You just can't be downhearted around Ernie. He is the best and I love him.

11

The Battle of the Budget

(and Other Hollywood Tidbits)

Ever since they've been making pictures, they've had a running battle with the budget, the estimate of how much the picture is going to cost in its final state. I don't care how much money you've got, whether it's a twenty-million-dollar picture, a fifty-million-dollar picture, or a one-million-dollar picture, all you'll ever hear is "the budget."

"It's not in the budget." "We don't have the money for it." "It's under-budget." "It's over-budget." It's *constantly* on everybody's mind. Which reminds me of a joke I heard.

In a zoo in a little town in the Midwest, there are two old lions, and one of them dies. The zookeepers get a new, young lion, and they put him in the cage next to the old lion's. The young lion paces back and forth in his cage, and when people come up to look at them, he roars. The old lion just lies around and sleeps all day. When it comes time to be fed, the old lion gets steaks, and big chunks of meat, and the young lion gets grapes, peanuts, and bananas.

This goes on for about a week, and finally the young lion goes over and pounds on the cage of the old lion. He says, "Old lion, all you do all day long is lie around and sleep and scratch yourself. I'm a young lion. I pace back and forth, and I roar at the crowd! But when it comes time to eat, they feed you big chunks of meat, and they give me peanuts, grapes, and bananas."

The old lion yawns, and he says, "Well, let me tell you, young fella. This is a low-budget zoo, and they've got you down on the books as a monkey."

❄   ❄   ❄   ❄   ❄

Come to think of it, on some of the pictures I've done, they must've had me down as a monkey, because I got peanuts.

I usually rave about the cost of pictures nowadays. Up until about ten years ago, the profits from *all* the pictures that were made in one year, the figure that those pictures could bring in domestically, in one year, was about a billion-six. This figure is much more now, but that's because the cost of the tickets has gone up.

For years, everybody was making pictures, trying to get part of that billion-six. That figure stayed pretty much the same for, I don't know . . . twenty-five years.

I always equate the picture business to the Indianapolis Speedway. When the 500 race first started, the prize was about a hundred thousand dollars. It only cost the car owners about twenty thousand to put a car in the race, and they could win a hundred thousand.

Now over the years at the Indianapolis Speedway, the prize money has gone up and up, so now you can win up to four or five million dollars. You can also spend much, much more on the cars.

For those many years in Hollywood, the prize was always a billion, six hundred million. The cost of the pictures kept going up, and the prize that you could win stayed the same. It just didn't make any sense. Today, we have pictures that cost a hundred, two hundred million dollars. Now granted, as I say, the pictures make much more a year than they did, but for many years, that gross was stuck on a number that should have kept people making pictures for a price that would allow them to come out ahead on the other end.

Nobody seemed to pay any attention to that. They just went right along raising the price of the picture. The unions got more and more, the actors got more and more and more. The picture companies actually make their money in distribution, because they get that money from the box office before anybody else has a chance to get their hands on it.

I remember once Paramount made a picture with Marlon Brando. They gave him 100 percent of the net, and they *still* made money because they were making 40 percent for distribution of the picture he made. With that 40 percent and other creative financing, the studios were able to do just fine.

They also make a mistake by hiring new directors who haven't done any pictures. It's as if you were going to build a ten-million-dollar house, and you went to a builder who had built a thousand ten-million-dollar houses, you gave him the plans, and you said, "Build a house." Well, that house will go up in the right amount of time, and you can keep the cost pretty much under control.

Whereas, if you took those plans and gave them to a guy who didn't even know how to read the plans, and he'd never built a house, he'll get the house done, it'll just take him four times longer than it would if he knew what he was doing. On-the-job training is costing the picture business an awful lot of money. In short, the inmates are running the asylum. What's the old saying? "Things aren't like they used to be, and they never were."

But on the whole, the young guard are doing a very good job. They've come out with some very good pictures, and they've finally discovered that a picture with heart, such as *Babe,* the little story of a pig, can walk away with a lot of money.

For a guy who knows as much about the motion picture business as I do, I made as many mistakes as anybody. It's all such a gamble, a guessing game. We're always trying to get on the bandwagon of a trend in pictures. Jack Warner, in the old days, said, "We don't make trend pictures. We *set* the trends at Warner Bros." And they did, if you'll remember, with the gangster pictures and the musicals and some of the great films like *The Maltese Falcon* and *Key Largo, High Sierra* and *The Treasure of the Sierra Madre.*

Speaking of *Treasure,* which I've said before is my favorite movie, Henry Blanke, the producer, told me that when they were down in Mexico making it Jack Warner was seeing the dailies and didn't like them at all. As a matter of fact, he didn't like them so much that he took his name off the picture. They had the Warner Bros. shield, and then at the bottom it always said, "Jack Warner in Charge of Production." He took that credit off. And it turned out to be one of the great, great movies.

The same thing happened to the great western writer named Bill Gulick. Bill had written a book called *Bend of the Snake,* and they made it over at Universal. Borden Chase, another famous western writer who had written *Red River,* did the script for *Bend of the Snake.* Borden told me that they changed the name of the picture to *Bend of the River.* Jimmy Stewart was in it, as was Arthur Kennedy. They made the picture, and Gulick read the Borden Chase script, and as most novelists would have reacted, didn't like the script because it had been changed from the novel and the title had been altered. So Bill Gulick took his name off the picture. Turned out to be one of the best westerns ever made.

On a panel I was once on, I was asked the question, "What's the hardest thing about writing a screenplay from a novel?" I said, "Facing the author after you've finished the script." Because they seldom like it. The reason being that you take a three- or four-hundred-page novel, and you have to do a hundred-and-twenty-page script. Right away, there's at least a hundred and eighty pages that are missing, and that doesn't sit well with the original author.

I tell the story about a picture I did called *Welcome to Hard Times,* from the E. L. Doctorow novel. He came out in the press saying that it was the second-worst picture he'd ever seen. I was afraid to ask him what the first one was. I was afraid it was one of mine.

Robert Ludlum, who's written a number of spy stories and high adventures, wrote a book called *The Rhineman Exchange.* It was over at Universal, and they told me that they were going to get Steve McQueen to play the leading man. Well, they had the first name right, but it ended up being Steve Collins. He's a good actor, but it wasn't Steve McQueen.

So we made it as a television show; I think it ran four or five hours. We filmed in Mexico. Ludlum said that when he read the script, which was by Richard Collins, he decided to leave the country when it played.

I got a break with a script that I did of a Louis L'Amour book: He died before the picture came out.

I think the only author who liked what I did with his work was Max Evans. Max wrote the novel *The Rounders*, which I made with Henry Fonda and Glenn Ford. Max and I have been friends ever since.

I think that's why I did so many originals when I first started in the business. *Seven Men from Now* was an original, as were *Ride Lonesome, Comanche Station*, and *Train Robbers*.

I truly can understand the author's position, because when I do a script and some actor changes his lines, I get furious. The late great Warren Oates used to say to me, "Why don't I say this instead of the way it's written?" I used to say, "Warren, say anything you can remember."

I guess you could say I'm mellowing, although, as I've said, there's a fine line between mellowing and not giving a shit. That of course is not true, because I still get a big thrill walking on a stage to make a movie. I get that same thrill today as I did the first day I ever walked on a set. If that ever changes, I guess I'll pack it in.

✿   ✿   ✿   ✿   ✿

Apropos of nothing, one of my other pet peeves in Hollywood is having to go to Guild meetings. They only happen once a year. The Writers Guild doesn't care if you show up or not, but the Directors Guild does. If you don't show up for the main meeting, they charge you a fifty-dollar penalty for not attending. Many times I've paid it just so I didn't have to sit through four hours of baloney.

One of the things they do every year at the Directors Guild meeting is all the members stand and they read off the names of the members who have passed away during the previous year. Last year I was standing with Denver Pyle. We listened to the names, and when they were finished, Denver said to me, "Every year I'm afraid my name is gonna be on that list."

The Writers Guild is a little more painless because they're kind of funny. I remember one year they were having a discussion about residuals. The residuals were not paid by the studios for anything that was made before 1960. From then on, they had to pay residuals to writers, directors, and actors. There were hundreds and hundreds of pictures made during the twenties, thirties, forties, and fifties, and any of those pictures are free. Anyone can just show it, and anything they get is profit.

The Guild was trying to remedy this somehow, and of course, they'd already signed the contract, so there's no way they could. But one old guy at the meeting, he must have been in his late eighties, stood up. He had on an old gray overcoat, and he said, "During the thirties I wrote fifteen scripts for pictures. They starred some of the biggest names in town." He said, "Because it was in the thirties, I don't get any residuals. I was one of the founding fathers of the Screenwriters Guild. As a matter of fact, when the Guild was first starting, they needed fifteen dollars to send out mailers to prospective members, and they didn't have the fifteen, so I gave it to them to send out the mail. I just feel that I go so far back with the Guild that it's wrong that I don't get residuals."

One of the young members got up and said, "Give him back his fifteen dollars."

On the subject of guilds in Hollywood, I've been a member of the Screenwriters Guild since 1952. In the forty-some years that I've been a member, I have walked the picket line on three separate strikes, and it is so amazing to see what happens to a bunch of people when they finally decide to strike against the producers. It's like, I guess, when people go to war. . . .

I remember, before the strike, I was called in to work on the phones and call members, and ask them what would be the best time for them to walk the picket line. I had eighty-five names to call, some of them very prominent writers, and not one volunteered to walk the picket line. The closest I came to getting a volunteer was on an answering machine: "I'm sorry, I'm not home, leave a message. . . ." Anyway, I got about halfway through it, then he broke in and said, "Okay, this is me. What can I do for you?"

I said, "This is Burt Kennedy, and I'm calling from the Guild to find out what is the best time for you to walk the picket line when we strike, in the morning or in the afternoon." The guy said, "Oh, this is a recording, too," and he hung up. That's the closest I came to getting anyone out on the picket line.

12

"Revenge

Is Sweet"

Years ago, when I first started writing, I was sent over to Gene
Autry's outfit. There was a production manager there named Lou
Gray. I'd been sent over for the possibility of being a writer for
Autry, who at the time had two or three series on the air.

I met with Lou Gray, and he was very nice, but he didn't hire
me. So now you dissolve thirty-five years. I'm a director at Metro,
and I'm doing the pilot of *The Rounders*. I had done the movie,
so when they did it as a TV series, I produced and directed the
TV pilot.

In the meantime, this Lou Gray, who had worked for Autry,
was now the head of television production at Metro. One day he
came into my office while we were preparing to make this pilot,
and he said to me, "You know, I knew a guy named Kennedy
years ago, a writer, skinny guy."

I was currently weighing in at two hundred pounds, but in those
long-ago days, I *was* skinny. I was an out-of-work, skinny writer.
All during the war I think I weighed a hundred and fifty pounds.

But he didn't leave it at that. He went on to say some bad things about this skinny writer named Kennedy of thirty-five years ago. I just listened to him. I didn't say anything.

There came a time in the show where the two cowboys who were playing the leads have their horse-truck parked in the street on the back lot at Metro. They got into some kind of trouble, and a fight starts.

They'd been in some kind of trouble before, and they didn't want to be connected with this fight, so they run across the street and get into their truck. Pat Wayne was one of the characters, and the script called for him to throw the truck in reverse and start to back up, then pull out and go screaming out of town.

What the characters didn't know when they jumped in the truck was that a police car had pulled up right behind them, and when Pat puts the truck in reverse, he backs up and runs into this brand-new police car.

Lou Gray was out there, and he said, "Burt, how're you going to do this thing where they're supposed to run into the police car and wreck it?"

I said, "Well, what I'll do is I'll just have Pat back up and then sort of react like he hit something, and then in the cutting, we'll see the truck backing up, then we'll take out one of the lights or something, maybe tracer paper, and make it look like he wrecked that police car."

Lou said, "Oh, good, good . . . I didn't want you to hurt that car, 'cause it's brand-new . . ."

I went over to Pat, and I said, "When you put it in reverse, *really* gun it. I want you to wipe that police car out!"

Pat loved it. I yelled, "Action!" Here they come . . . running across the street, and we see the police car pull up behind the truck. They jump in. Pat starts the truck, and he backs up and absolutely wipes out this brand-new police car.

Lou Gray was standing there, and he said, "Now I remember who that skinny writer was." And he turned around and just walked away, shaking his head.

✳   ✳   ✳   ✳   ✳

Production people are pretty much all the same—they just don't want you to spend money. When I was doing the TV series *Simon & Simon,* the producer was a great guy named John Stevens, but he just didn't want you to spend any money.

We were doing a show and we had to have a car that the bad guys had stolen and repainted. There was a scene in this paint shop where they were drying the car after they'd painted it, and it was like an oven. It wasn't very visual, so I said to the art director, "What if we put some red neon strips along the walls, and up above the ceiling, and down the other side, so it looks like we've got the car in a toaster."

John Stevens came roaring in and he said, "Burt, that'd cost a lot of money! This isn't a feature, you know."

I said, "Yeah, John, and it isn't a radio show either. We gotta spend *some* money!" But it was always like pulling teeth.

Another big spender, who is a dear friend of mine and has been for many years, is Bill Finnegan. He, too, hates to spend money. One time we were going out on a location hunt in Conejo, California, or someplace. We were about ten people, including the cameraman, the gaffer, the art director, and a number of other people.

I should mention here that one of the perks in television is that when you go out on these location hunts away from the studio, it is an unwritten law that you stop at some nice place and have lunch. I think Universal made a rule whereby you had to be three miles away from the front gate in order to do this.

But on this particular bus ride, Finnegan had decided he could save a lot of money if instead of stopping for lunch with these ten guys, he'd bring it along. He'd had Pat, his wife, make up a bunch of peanut butter sandwiches, and he had some warm Cokes. When it came time for lunch, he dug out this brown paper bag full of peanut butter sandwiches. You talk about a mutiny! All Bill said was, "Well, it was worth a try." Then he gave in and took us to a nice restaurant.

I don't know why production managers or producers ever fool with a director, 'cause he can stick a knife in the production company, and they won't even feel it go in.

For instance, when I was in Brackettville, Texas, doing the TV remake *The Alamo*, the set was the one that Wayne had built. About forty of the cast members were staying in Del Rio, which was about an hour by bus from the set. Because our contracts are always portal-to-portal, we'd have to start paying from the time they got on the bus until they got off the bus at the end of the day.

One of the production people came to me and said, "You know, we could save a lot of time and money if we moved those actors from Del Rio." They were at a Holiday Inn, very nice place, swimming pool and all. He said, "Move 'em up to Fort Clark," which was this *terrible* place that some of the crew, like the art directors and a few others, were staying. But they at least had pretty nice quarters. The *regular* quarters were like barracks that soldiers used to stay in—in 1888. He said, "Well, we'll put 'em in those places."

I thought, Well, that isn't going to work, but I just let them go blithely on about their business. One night we finished work and the production people made the announcement to the actors on the bus that they were not going to be taken back to Del Rio and that their belongings had been moved from this motel in Del Rio to these cells in Fort Clark.

They bused them over to the fort. I was staying at Clark, in luxury apartments at the back of the Army post, as were Alec Baldwin, Jim Arness, my assistant Ray Marsh, and some others. We were fine. We even had a golf course. It was wonderful, but for the peons, it was awful.

They moved the actors into these terrible places. One of the rooms didn't even have a window. I said to Ray Marsh, "Let's go have a drink." The fort had a bar down in the middle of the camp, and I said, "Let's go down there," because I knew what was going to happen.

We went into the bar, and all these actors who had been bused over to the barracks were having a drink and they wouldn't even look at me. They thought *I* was the one who had made this decision. On the way to the bar I had seen Gene Evans on a pay phone, surrounded by fellow actors, screaming.

We ordered a drink, and in came Gene, and he roared, "Burt, do you know what they've done to us?"

I said, "Yeah."

He yelled, "You can't do that to us! Buck Taylor doesn't even have a window in his room!" They were all screaming complaints, and Gene said, "What're you gonna do about it?"

The production gal was there, and she said, "Yeah, what *are* we gonna do?"

I said, "You're gonna get the bus, put 'em on it, and take 'em back to Del Rio." That's what they did, and the mutiny was over.

That incident reminded me of what John Huston used to say, which I thought was a perfect line. When he would do something stupid, and people would ask, "Why did you do that?" his answer would be, "I did it because it was the *wrong* thing to do."

Huston also said, "On a picture, you do everything wrong before you do it right."

✦   ✦   ✦   ✦   ✦

In talking about Gene Evans at *The Alamo* fiasco, I was reminded that Sam Fuller made Evans famous in a picture called *The Steel Helmet* in 1951. Gene was nominated for an Oscar, and it was one of his first pictures. He's a dear friend of mine, but you wouldn't know it from what I did.

I was doing *The War Wagon,* and Gene was in it. While we were down in Mexico, they were also making a TV series, *Tarzan.* There were real short budgets, so what they'd do was, if there was a picture being made in Mexico City or thereabouts, and there was an actor in that production they could use, they'd hire him, and when he finished whatever picture he was on, he'd just stay on and do the television show, and that way they saved a plane fare coming down from Hollywood.

Anyway, these producers wanted Gene Evans to do two episodes of *Tarzan.* So Gene came to me, and he said, "Now, Burt, they gave me these two scripts, and they're terrible. There's one of them where I carry a guy on my back through the jungle for about a week. And in another one, I wrestle with an alligator. I don't want to do it, so I've told them that I'm not going to finish when I was supposed to, that I was going to have to work three more weeks. So, if they come out on the set and ask you, tell them that there's been a change of plans and you have to keep me on the picture, and that way I won't be able to do these two ball-breaker television shows."

We were doing a big saloon fight, and these two producers came on the set. I was going to finish with Gene that night, and they knew it. So they came on the set to make sure that Gene could start work the next day on their television show.

When they arrived, they said, "You're finishing with Gene Evans today . . ." That was when I was supposed to say, "No, we need him for another month." But I said, "Yeah, I finish with him in probably about an hour!"

Well, poor Gene had to stay in Mexico for about three more weeks and do these two shows, after we had gone home, and I've never heard the end of it. He's a wonderful guy with a great sense of humor. He hasn't gotten back at me yet . . . but he will.

13

Animals

I did a two-hour television show a few years ago called *Down the Long Hills* and it featured a grizzly bear. This bear later became famous in a picture called *The Bear*. His name is Bart, and he belongs to a trainer in Utah named Doug Seuss. We had scenes with the bear where he comes up to a horse and he fights with Indians. He's an amazing trained bear.

Sometimes animals are kept in an area which is hot-wired. A live wire is strung up with enough voltage to shock the animals if they touch it. They eventually learn to stay away from the wire, and usually will not cross it.

My first assistant, Ray Marsh, is a dear friend and a great guy, but he loves to give speeches to the crew and visitors on the set. One of his big speeches at night is, "Don't look into the arc lights. It can burn the retina. . . ." He goes on and on for ten minutes about burning the retina.

One day, we were working with Bart the bear, and it was a touchy situation. Ray Marsh got up to give his speech to the crowd, warning them of the dangers of a runaway bear. He emphasized that if the bear should break away from his trainer, everyone should stand perfectly still and not move at all. If you run, he told the assembled, the bear will chase you.

Well, the bear got loose and everybody ran. They caught the bear and everyone was fine, fortunately. After that whenever we'd get ready to do a scene with a rabbit, the crew would say, "Now be very careful. If the rabbit breaks loose, it can be very dangerous and you should stand still." We did a scene with a trout in a river and someone would say, "Now, if the trout gets away from the trainer, don't move. There's nothing worse than a runaway trout."

I'm an animal lover, especially dogs. I'm not talking about some of the pictures I made, I'm talking about the dogs I've owned over the years. I figured it out one day. I've had just over fifty.

The first dog I remember was in Michigan when I was a kid at Wolf Lake. He was a German shepherd named Bluejay. He was with my brother and me everywhere we went. When we would stay on the other side of the lake too long some nights, and it would get dark, and we couldn't find our way home, we'd hold on to his collar and he'd bring us right to the front door. He was with us all the time. I don't think we "owned" him; I don't think *anybody* owned him. I just think he bummed around, but mostly he was with us.

When I moved to Ravenna, Michigan, I had many hunting dogs. One of them was a little beagle, and she had pups.

I should mention here that another dog we had before that ate some meat poisoned with strychnine that one of our ornery old bastard neighbors had dropped off. He was in the throes of death. My stepdad, who knew everything about everything (I don't know how, but he did), took a Coke bottle and filled it up with kerosene and lard. Then he picked up the dog and shoved the bottle down her throat, and let all this stuff drain into her.

He turned her loose and said, "Now leave her alone, just leave her alone; don't go near her. Just cover her up with a blanket and leave her alone."

So, I thought I had a dead dog. I put her in the garage with a blanket over her. I thought she was a goner.

The next morning I came out to check on her, and she was out running around in the field next to our house. She was fine from then on.

Getting back to that little beagle who had the puppies . . . This guy who had poisoned my other dog did the same thing to her. She was nursing these pups, and she got ahold of some of this strychnine. She died, and so did all the pups.

I had a four-ten shotgun. I went in the house and loaded it. I knew who this guy was, and I knew exactly what I was gonna do. I was going to his house, and when he opened the door, I was going to shoot him. It was very simple. I was very calm. I had decided I was gonna blow this guy away. He deserved it.

My all-knowing stepdad saw me come out the door with the shotgun. He had seen what had happened with the pups, and he knew where I was headed. He very calmly explained to me why shooting this guy was not the right thing to do, and he talked the gun away from me. Otherwise, I *know* I would have shot this guy.

During the war, of course, I didn't have a dog. But when I came out to California, I had a whole bunch of them. The first one I had was a little toy poodle named Corky, who was a little devil. He had belonged to a very good actress named Peggy Dowe, from Oklahoma; she later married an oilman and got out of the business. My wife and I decided that since we had Corky, we should also have a girl poodle, so we got a miniature. Poucette, which means "flealet" and Corky mated. Poucette had five pups. We sold three of them and kept two—one we called Miss Brown, because she was brown, and another one we named Shitty, because he had rolled in some out on the lawn.

It was funny, when the kids were in school, if they were ever asked about him, he was "Shitty" in the backyard and "Smitty" in the front yard and at school. We had those dogs for years and years.

Then we had a little toy poodle called Too Much and a pointer spaniel named Howdy. We got a divorce and my wife Sue got

Howdy in the settlement. She took him to Oklahoma, and he was there for years, running loose.

Then I was doing a picture up in Kanab, Utah, and on the picture was the wife of one of the wranglers, Rose Lundine, a wonderful gal. Her husband, Richard Lundine, drives the stagecoach in all the Wells Fargo television ads; you've probably seen him. Rose had this little Queensland Heeler whose mother and father had been champions down in Cedar Springs . . . or Cedar something. . . .

I wanted to buy the little dog. She said "All right—fifty dollars on the barrelhead." So I gave her the fifty bucks, and I brought Belle home, and she was with me until she died, about thirteen years later. But with Belle, we also bought a dog, a Doberman, called Finnegan. The reason I called him Finnegan was because there was a producer who was once my first assistant and a friend, and his name was Finnegan. Actually, he was German, but he'd been adopted by a family named Finnegan, so he was Bill Finnegan. This was a German dog, so I named him Finnegan. He was with us for years—a wonderful dog.

Finnegan died and I got another Doberman named Timber. The reason we called her Timber was because she had narcolepsy. When she'd get excited about anything, she'd go into this catatonic state, and then she'd snap out of it. The breeders wanted us to put her to sleep when we first got her, but she was so sweet, and we kept her. She had that narcolepsy until the day she passed away, but otherwise she was fine.

Then I had my love, Gertie, who was a little Scottie, and whom I had for thirteen and a half years. She died tragically. I took her to the vet's one day, and a guy was getting out of a car with a rottweiler—or, as I call him, a "rotten weiler." The dog broke loose from the guy and he attacked my Gertie. He hurt her so bad, I had to put her to sleep, and it almost killed me. I have nightmares about it still.

Then, to replace Gertie, I got another black Scottie. Now, Gertie had been named after my mother, Gertrude, and so I named this one after my dad, Thomas James. We call him Tommy or T. J., and he's a marvelous dog. I've had him for about five years.

Then I got another dog, a pal for Tommy. She's Amy, and she's a Westie. They're like Scotties, only they're more hyper and they bark a lot. As a matter of fact, Tommy never barked for three years, never once, until Amy came to live with us. Now he barks all the time.

I seem to have strayed well off the subject of Hollywood, but my dogs are more important than anything that's ever happened to me making pictures.

14

Comedy

Years ago, when I first got out here to Hollywood, I was at lunch over at a restaurant called Lucy's. It was a very famous restaurant across from the gates of Paramount and a lot of the stars used to go over there for lunch. I ended up there one day with Buster Keaton and a group of other people. We were talking about comedy. I remembered him from when I was a little kid. He used to come out to Wolf Lake, Michigan, a resort where I lived. He would come in the summertime with his sister, though I don't think she was in the business. I remember that he drove a fancy car.

Then, these many years later, I was sitting there with him at Lucy's, and we were talking about what works in comedy, and what doesn't, and he told me a story. He said that most comics who were successful in the early days got so successful that they had their own studios, and their own companies. Guys like Chaplin. Buster had a company where he made his own films. Harold Lloyd did the same thing. I don't think Jerry Lewis ever had a studio, but he had his company. Maybe because they were comics they didn't think anybody took them seriously, and had to build studios to convince everybody they knew what they were doing.

Anyway, we were talking about comedy, and Buster said, "I was doing a picture, and the gag was that I had talked my way into being a waiter on a dining car. It was a very fancy dining car, and I didn't know anything about being a waiter. All these fancy-dressed people came into the dining car, and I was to take their orders and serve them. I was to get all mixed up in the orders, and finally I was to end up by spilling things on people and just completely making a mess out of the dining car, a complete shambles. I did the trick where I pull the tablecloth out from under the dishes, but the dishes went all over the car, and it was just a mess, just absolutely tore up everything. When we were shooting it, everybody thought it was funny.

"We took it to the theater, and nobody laughed. They didn't think it was funny." So he said, "I thought, I wonder what's the matter with this thing." He went back, put an actor in a conductor's uniform, and placed him at the end of the car, standing just inside the door of the dining room. He was watching Buster do all these shenanigans, and was reacting with pained expressions. Buster cut that into the sequence, then took it back out to the theaters. Now, because there was somebody reacting to it, it gave the audience a chance to laugh at it, and they did. It was a riot. He said, "I learned a lesson from that." I think what he was really saying is that you have to have a straight man.

I've found that when you're doing comedies—for instance, comedy-westerns, of which I've done quite a few—you have to have one guy in the picture, preferably the leading man, who is completely straight. The whole town, everybody around him, can be crazy, absolutely out of their minds, but he has to be straight. And he doesn't really "get it." He doesn't think anything's particularly funny, even as the other people go wild. And that works—it's worked for me a number of times, like in *Support Your Local Sheriff*.

When it *doesn't* work is when *everybody* in the picture's crazy. This was the case with *Dirty Dingus Magee*, where everyone was a comic and there was no straight man—except the audience, who didn't think it was funny. You need one guy in a picture who . . . well, take George Burns.

You know, Gracie without George Burns wouldn't have worked. You have to have that straight man. On occasion I've forgotten that, and when I do, the picture usually goes in the toilet.

Comedy can be very dangerous to a picture if it isn't done right. There's a wonderful picture that Stanley Kramer made called *Oklahoma Crude.* Jack Palance played the hangdog heavy, and George C. Scott, John Mills, and Faye Dunaway were in it. It was a really great movie, except that Stanley couldn't make up his mind whether he wanted to do a comedy or a straight drama. There's an action sequence at the end of the picture where the bad guys charge this oil well up on top of the hill, and Stanley did what amounted to a half-comic, half-for-real fight. It confused the audience, so they didn't know whether to laugh or groan. I think that kept it from being one of the best pictures that Stanley ever made, and he made a lot of good ones. Henry Mancini did the score, and it was one of the best scores for a picture I've ever heard. There were some wonderful scenes between Scott and Dunaway in the picture, too. But comedy can be dangerous.

I think another reason why I remember that picture is the writer, Marc Norman. Though it was his initial film, he got more money for the *Oklahoma Crude* script than I made in the first twenty years that I was in Hollywood. I'll always remember that, too—and that's *not* funny.

That reminds me of a Gary Cooper joke. Somebody said to Cooper years ago that he didn't have a sense of humor, and Cooper said, "I like a joke as well as the next man—just so it ain't too funny."

Cooper was notoriously cheap. He loved cars, had all sorts. One time he decided to drive across the country from California to New York. So he took his checkbook along, and every time he would stop at a station to get gas, he'd write a check for it. Of course, the station attendants never cashed the checks, they framed them! So the checks were never paid off, and it didn't cost Cooper anything to drive across country. Not a bad idea.

✤   ✤   ✤   ✤   ✤

Another movie star who was frugal was Fred MacMurray. I remember writer John Lee Mahin used to go duck hunting with Clark Gable and Fred MacMurray up in Bakersfield, California. There was some marshland up there, and this outfit had built some duck blinds. They would drive up there in the middle of the night so that they could be in the blinds at dawn. John Lee said that they'd get into the blinds at about five o'clock in the morning, when it was still dark, and then stay there till almost noon.

Gable and John always carried a little paper bag with their lunch, fried chicken and whatever, and they had a thermos of coffee. MacMurray would never bring anything. When they'd start to eat, they'd feel a bit guilty, and they'd say, "Fred, aren't you hungry?" And he'd say, "Well, no, I'll just eat whatever you leave." And that's exactly what he did.

✤   ✤   ✤   ✤   ✤

There was another guy like that, and he wasn't that big a star, but he was funny. His name was John Russell. He was a western star, and he had a long period where he didn't work and he was broke. Finally he got a job, the lead in a series over at Warner Bros., *The Lawman*. He was making good money now, but John had been broke for so long, he never forgot the fact that he'd been down-and-out. He would come to the studio with a brown bag with some peanut butter sandwiches, and when they'd break for lunch, he'd go into the commissary, sit down and order some water, and open up his little brown bag, and while everybody else was having the "chef's special" John would eat his peanut butter sandwiches.

Glenn Ford used to throw money around like a guy with no arms, but I think he got over that. He made a ton of money and had a career that went for forty-five, almost fifty years. He still lives in a beautiful home behind the Beverly Hills Hotel. It's a gorgeous place. I was just there recently on his eightieth birthday.

I guess he figured that since he was gonna live to a ripe old age, he'd better hang on to some of his dough.

Picture people being cheap doesn't bother me at all unless they happen to be production managers or producers. That can get you in so much trouble. I remember I was doing my first picture in Canada, and we had a production manager (now they call them "line producers"). We had a scene where we had five hundred Indians, and we had to build an Indian camp. This production manager came to me, and he said, "You know, these Indian tepees cost a lost of money. They're made out of deer hide. I have this great idea. Rather than do them with hides, which are expensive, let's go to the stores and buy brown wrapping paper, and we'll just wrap it around the poles, and nobody will ever know the difference. We can paint on some Indian figures—you know, feathers and horses. We'll save twenty-five thousand dollars."

I should have known then what was going to happen. He brought in these five hundred Indians. I don't know what they were, Sioux, I think, the ones who had crossed over into Canada after the Little Bighorn. They arrived in ten buses. They dumped them off in the middle of this field, and this production manager had made no provisions for taking care of them. They didn't have any food, they didn't have any water, no tents, nothing.

The Indians were upset, and they decided they weren't just going to camp out in the middle of a field and starve, so they built some huts out of tree branches and so on, and then some of the braves went out hunting and shot some antelope for food. So the first night, they had a big barbecue; all of them came to this big encampment. They built a big fire, and according to some of our assistants, they did a war dance asking the Indian gods to scalp this production manager, who was again saving money.

Next day he brought them water and food, because he really believed they were going to kill him. But getting back to this money he saved on the encampment that he was building with wrapping paper. . . .

There were about seventy-five or eighty tepees, and we had little fires around in various places in the camp. I was way up on a hillside with a bunch of cameras, and the gag was that we'd see this camp, and then we'd see these riders move on, and they'd play the scene. The assistants were dressed up like Indians so they could be right in the camp, and their job was to start the fires when we were ready to roll. There must have been at least twenty or thirty little campfires, scattered through the camp.

We rolled the cameras and told the assistants to light the fires. There was a wind blowing, and the fires caught on to the grass, and we started a grass fire in the encampment and it got out of control. As it swept through the camp, the Indians ran. It wasn't really dangerous, they were just getting out of the way of the fire. It lit up all of these wrapping-paper tepees. When they caught fire, they burned from the bottom up, and when they did, this wrapping paper sort of rose to the sky in circles as it unwound from these tepees, and I had seventy-five tepees wafting in the air. Well, I thought it was funny, because I knew this guy had tried to save money, and I started laughing, and the whole camp went up!

The production manager, in trying to save twenty-five thousand, cost himself seventy-five to build a real camp, which we shot about two weeks later. We should have shot the production manager.

The secret of making pictures is knowing where to spend the money. If a studio can find one or two people to intelligently run the production department, they can have a very successful operation.

Of course, there are problems with personalities. You have many people who are very good at production, but get carried away. Everybody in the picture business wants to be somebody else. The production manager wants to be an executive . . . wants to be a director . . . wants to be—and that can get them in a lot of trouble. But there are some very good production managers in this town.

One is William Finnegan. When I first met him, he was my second assistant on *The Rounders,* which I made in Sedona, Arizona, in 1964. The next time we came together was on *Support Your Local Sheriff* in 1968. Bill had worked his way up to where he was a production manager. When we made *Support Your Local Gunfighter* in 1972, I made Bill the producer.

It was so funny. We had a little run-in before the picture started, because Bill, like most people, had a little trouble wearing the star at first. In other words, when you've been an assistant director, and all of a sudden you're the producer of a picture, it kind of goes to your head. So we had a little go-around where I had to tell him off—that I had put him in the chair, and that he was great, but that I was still the guy who made the picture.

I was finishing another picture at Metro when I had this meeting with Bill where he went around and around a little, and he sent me a ten-page resignation. It was on a yellow legal tablet, and I read it. It said how he was only trying to do his job, and he was hurt because I'd gotten on him a little. Anyway, it went on and on for ten pages, so I wrote back a note, and I said I wouldn't accept his resignation.

We went ahead, and we made *Support Your Local Gunfighter*, and then Bill went on from there to be a very, very successful producer. He had his own production company that did long-form television shows and movies. And what Bill had, and his company had, was that he could go to a studio, and if they wanted to do a project that was going to cost them say four or five million dollars, Bill could do it for three. So he would take over these projects, and do them for the studios, and he became very, very successful.

We came together again in the late eighties. I did a western for Bill up in Utah, for Disney. And then we did the television version of *The Alamo*. Where John Wayne had seven thousand Mexicans to storm the Alamo, I had seventy-five, so I decided to do the big battle at night—and it actually happened just before dawn so it worked out pretty good for a television show, and that's the last time we worked together. But I see him all the time, and he's a wonderful guy, and a great producer.

One of the perks when you're directing films is you have a makeup and hair department that you can call upon to give you a free haircut whenever you need one.

I was in Spain making *The Return of the Seven* with Yul Brynner in 1965. I hadn't had a haircut for three months, and I looked pretty shaggy. One day at lunch I asked the hair department if I could get a clip.

Instead of a haircut, I got an "ear-cut"—the barber accidentally cut the top of my ear off. Everybody panicked when they saw blood streaming down my neck, except for the stuntmen, who laughed like hell.

The first aid man patched me up and I went back to work. There was a bullfight scene in the film. The following Sunday our matador fought at the Alicante bullring and did so well he was awarded two ears and a tail. He presented them to Yul, who was the guest of honor that night.

When I got back to the Carlton Hotel, where we were all staying, there was an envelope in my mailbox. Inside of the envelope was one of the bull's ears that had been presented to Yul, with a note to me saying, "Use mine!"

Yul Brynner had a great sense of humor and was a complete delight on the film.

The last time I saw him was at the airport in Madrid. He put his arms around me and said, "God bless you, Burt." I said, "God Bless? I thought you were a Buddhist."

We had a last laugh together and he was gone. I've missed him ever since.

I don't know about you, but I hate to be told what to do. Maybe it is because of all the time I spent in the Army, but I just hate it. Like when I get a bill, and there is a return envelope, and up in the right-hand corner it says "Place stamp here." I mean, I get furious. And of course, that lapped over into my picture business.

I remember Randy Scott told me years ago, "Coming events cast their shadows." He was talking about my gaining weight, and he was right, but I've always remembered that phrase, and whenever I get into a situation where something is going on that I know is just the beginning of what's *really* gonna happen, I walk away.

For instance, I was doing tests for a picture called *Skin Game* with Jim Garner over at Warner Bros. I was testing for the black slave in the picture. I was testing Lou Gossett Jr. (who finally got the part), Cleavon Little, and another gentleman. We were on a stage, and we had a horse tied to a log by a campfire, and Jim was there, and the black man was to come up to him and play the scene.

We were in Panavision—that's the wide, wide screen—and I put the camera by the campfire on Jim. The producer of the picture came up to me and said, "I think the camera ought to go over here." I remembered Randy Scott's line, and I just got up, went out, and got in my car and went home.

I've done that on a number of occasions. I remember one at Universal, I was about to do a pilot. This producer found a microphone up in a booth way up at the top of the set, and at one point, he said on the loudspeaker, all over the set, "Put Kennedy on the earphone so I can tell him what to do."

Well, I handed the earphones to the assistant, and I told the producer what *he* could do and I went out and got into my car and went home. They called and said they were sorry, and I told them I hadn't done it for effect, I did it because I knew this was just the beginning of what was really going to happen later on in the picture, and I didn't want any part of it.

I guess that over the years those stories have gone around town. Frank Wells, as I remember, started off at some law firm as one of Jim Garner's lawyers, on *Support Your Local Sheriff*. He worked his way up to where he was very big at Paramount, and then he went over with Mike Eisner to Disney, and he was a big shot there. He kept saying around town that I was irresponsible. That was because, I think, I turned down the directing job on *Skin Game.* I got off that picture, and they put in the trades that I was a bad guy, and so on. That, coupled with my dear Italian friend Dino De Laurentiis, put me out of business for a while, but not forever.

Poor Frank Wells got killed in a helicopter crash. He was skiing up in Utah or someplace—a terrible tragedy. He was a very talented guy, and a good lawyer, but he didn't like me. What can I tell you?

I guess this comes under the heading of "studio bashing," but the story is going around that there's such a dearth of material at MGM that when an executive dies, at the end of his or her obituary it says, "In lieu of flowers, send story ideas to the Story Department at MGM, 10202 Washington Blvd., Culver City."

That kind of thinking pretty much goes along with what I feel about New Line Pictures. They have a talent detector on the front door and it hasn't gone off in ten years.

15

Cameramen

The first cameraman I ever had was Arthur Ibbetson, a very famous British cinematographer. He worked for David Lean on *Lawrence of Arabia.*

Arthur was an operator before he became a cameraman. On the standard, old Mitchell camera there was a finder that was off to the side of the camera which the operator would look through. It showed the exact screen that you would see after the film was developed. *Lawrence of Arabia* was the first picture he ever did in CinemaScope, which has a long drawn-out frame that a lot of cameramen say is only good for trains and snakes.

The first time he used this camera, he had a scene with George Sanders. George came into the bedroom, walked across the room, opened a dresser drawer, took out a gun, closed the drawer, crossed back, and went out the door. That was the scene.

"Action" was called. George came in and went across the room, got the gun, and crossed back out. Even though Arthur had been looking through the finder and not the lens, he did not realize that what he saw then was not what would be seen on film. When they saw the dailies, they didn't see the door open; all they saw was George walk across the room. They didn't see the drawer where he got the gun; all they saw was George walk across the room and walk back with a gun in his hand and he was gone. Arthur admitted he would have to get used to that lens.

❖   ❖   ❖   ❖   ❖

After I worked with Arthur, my next project was a television show at Warners, with Bert Glennon as my cameraman. Bert was one of the great old-time cameramen—cranky as can be. He was John Ford's cameraman for years.

We were doing this show and about halfway through it Bert came up to me and said, "You don't look through the camera enough."

I replied, "Every time I look through it, it's perfect."

He came back, "Yeah, but you won't have me as the cameraman all the time."

He was right, of course, about looking through the camera.

The next guy I had was really a cranky guy, Curly Lyndon. He was a drunk who was hung over most of the time, but a fabulous cameraman. He won several Academy Awards.

The first picture I did with Curly was the ninety-minute *Virginian*. We drove out to the location together. He didn't say a word and I didn't say a word to him. When we started, he said, "Well, whatta you want?" I told him what I wanted on the first setup. After the sixth or seventh setup, he started to talk to me.

I asked his operator, "What's with Curly?"

He said, "Well, he's sobering over. He can't really talk until about ten o'clock in the morning."

He was a wonderful cameraman. He's gone now, but he was wonderful—cranky but wonderful.

I then worked with a gentleman at Metro—I did two or three pictures with him—named Paul Vogel. He won an Academy Award for *Battleground*, which Bill Wellman directed. He was an old-timer and very good. His brother was Joe Vogel, who was the president of MGM, which didn't hurt his position too much. He did have the problem of not being able to explain to his crew what he wanted, and then he'd get mad because they wouldn't do what he'd told them to do.

Off the set, he was the nicest man you'd ever met, but when we'd get on the set, he'd get mad at the crew for doing something wrong. He was from the old school, and he stayed that way until the end.

A very good cameraman I worked with when I did the *Combat* series was Robert Hauser. He was actually great, but he had a little problem with the actors, because he treated them kind of like cattle. When he was ready for the actors, he'd say things like, "Open the cage and let 'em out." He didn't play the game too well, and consequently, he never became a very successful cameraman.

I latched up with Harry Stradling Jr., who was the son of a very famous cameraman, Harry Stradling. Harry and I did about eight pictures together. He was wonderful and still is. He is semiretired now, but he does a lot of pictures with Blake Edwards. He's been nominated a couple of times, once for *Little Big Man* with Dustin Hoffman. He's just a fabulous cameraman. We worked together so much, we didn't have to talk. When he followed me around, he knew where I wanted the camera and all of a sudden it was there. We had a language all our own.

I did two or three pictures with Bill Clothier, a famous cameraman who did all Wellman's, Wayne's, and Ford's films. As a matter of fact, he did the last big picture of mine, *The Train Robbers*, and then retired.

Since then I've used some really good younger cameramen. One was Ken Lamkin, who is still working all the time, and John Elsenbach, who did the television show *The Alamo* with me and got nominated for an Emmy. He, too, is a wonderful cameraman.

When I went to television, I worked with many great cameramen. On *Simon & Simon*, it was Brad May, who is now a very good director. He works as the cameraman and the director and sometimes even operates the camera himself—quite a bargain for the television people, especially since he is very talented.

Lloyd Ahern was an operator of the *Simon* shows and now has graduated into big pictures. He did *Geronimo* and *Wild Bill*. He's on his way—in orbit, in fact. He's a wonderful cameraman and a wonderful guy. When he was younger he was kind of a beatnik, with long hair and all . . . a real gentle person.

A funny story: He was over in Hawaii doing *Hawaii Five-O* with Jack Lord. They were doing a scene and Jack Lord was very taken with himself. He got upset with something and started yelling at one of the extras or crew members. Lloyd, who is really a gentle guy, came out from behind the camera and went over to Lord and grabbed him and said, "Don't talk to people like that!"

Lord knocked Lloyd down, jumped on top of him, grabbed him by the throat, and started choking him, saying, "You're fired! Get off *my* island!"

Another story about Jack Lord took place when I was doing a show for Bill Finnegan, who used to be the producer of *Hawaii Five-O*. Bill had a lot of trouble with Jack Lord. We were preparing to do a show and in keeping with a Hawaiian tradition, a native high priest came over to bless the project. It was supposed to be good luck.

Well, Jack Lord heard that Bill Finnegan, his ex-producer, was going to do a show which was in competition with *Hawaii Five-O*—it was called *Big Hawaii*. The day the high priest came over to bless our show, Jack Lord sent a higher priest over to put a curse on the show. And it worked! I think we were on the air for three shows and gone. His name isn't "Lord" for nothing.

Back to another cameraman, Alex Phillips Jr., whose father was one of the founders of the cameramen's union. He was doing a picture in Mexico and while there he met a Mexican girl and married her. I think Alex was Russian; anyway, he worked for his dad for many years in the Mexican film industry. He then started working here in town.

I used him on a television show in Mexico and afterward we went to Spain to make *The Trouble with Spies*.

When I suggested Alex to the people who put up the completion bond for the film, they objected because they had heard he had been drinking a lot. I said I didn't know about that, but I was kind of like his father, and believe me, he wouldn't drink on a picture with me.

He got the job and the first day he was drunk. Luckily, we had started on a Saturday, just to do some pickup shots in Ibiza, an island off the coast of Spain near Barcelona, so he had the weekend to sober up. He stayed sober for about five weeks. Then one morning we left for work about six o'clock in the morning and he was real talkative. I realized he was loaded.

He got on the set and Donald Sutherland was the star. Donald was complaining about some kind of lens Alex was using. When the cameraman used to ask me "What lens should I use?" I'd say, "The clean one." Donald was trying to tell Alex that the lens he was using was very bad for him, that it made him look old. So Alex started in on him, saying things like, "I will not make you look like a pumpkin; I know what I'm doing." He went on to say, "You're ruining this picture; you're no good" and they went on and on.

Finally Donald took me off to the side and said, "I can't work with a cameraman who thinks I'm no good."

I said, "But Donald, he's a drunk."

Donald said, "Oh, okay."

We managed to get through the day, while Donald kept insisting Alex be fired. That night we got back to the apartment complex where we were living in Madrid and I got a call from Donald. He and Alex were together and they were having a few, and now Donald took the position that under no circumstances would Alex be dismissed from the picture. If Alex were dismissed, Donald insisted, he would quit. Drunken loyalty.

That was the last time I worked with Alex. He's a fantastic cameraman, was one of Sam Peckinpah's favorites. He used to wear a derby hat . . . he had long blond hair down to his shoulders and this derby hat. Sam used to call him "the Golden Taco" and that name has stuck with him to this day.

16

Stuntmen

Yakima Canutt was the first stuntman who was ever recognized as a tremendous talent. He was a rodeo rider when he was a kid, and I don't know how he got into the picture business, but somehow he got here. He taught John Wayne how to fight—picture fights—and he did the famous stuff in *Stagecoach*, where he played an Indian. He jumps on a team of the six-ups pulling a stagecoach as it is being attacked by Indians. Wayne supposedly shoots him, he falls down between the running horses, and he's dragged along and finally lets go. The horses run right over him and the stagecoach goes over him and then he gets up, so you know it wasn't a fake. That is probably one of the most famous stunts that has ever been done in the picture business.

He had two wonderful sons who are great stuntmen, Joe and Tap Canutt. There are so many more. Buzz Henry, who was with me early on when I made pictures, and Jerry Gatlin, whom I trained to be a second-unit director. He's one of the best and is doing very well as a stunt coordinator. David Cass, who got smart and stopped doing stunts and started becoming an actor. He's been successful but he still does second units. He's done many for me—just excellent. There's Billy Burton, who was one of the top stuntmen in town. And Jackie Williams, who is now a millionaire and landowner, but had one of the great falling horses in the western business.

Then there was Good Chuck and Bad Chuck. Good Chuck was Chuck Hayward and Bad Chuck was Chuck Roberson. They worked with John Ford for many years. Bad Chuck doubled for Wayne for a lot of years.

They tell a tall story about one of the leading men in the silents. His name was Cliff Lyons. When the talking pictures came in, he had this squeaky little voice, so he couldn't be an actor anymore. He started doing stunts and he became very famous as a stunt coordinator and second-unit director. He did one of the famous stunts. A horse and rider are on a cliff—it must be about eighty-five feet high—and the horse jumps off. The rider then steps off to one side and they both hit the water, side by side. It's a magnificent stunt.

The way it happened was that they couldn't get a horse just to jump off a cliff, so they built a teeterboard. They put the horse on one end of it and they counterbalanced it with bags of sand. They balanced it so that the weight of the two stuntmen was what was keeping the horse and rider—Cliff—level. When they stepped off the end of the teeter-totter, the horse and rider slid down, right on down the hill and into the air.

It was a very dangerous stunt, and Cliff was very nervous. He got up on the horse. Good Chuck and Bad Chuck were sitting on the back of the teeterboard. I think they had greased the board under the horse so that when the board tilted downward, the horse just slid right off the edge of the cliff. They'd start the cameras down below and just as they'd get ready for the boys to step off the board, Cliff would say, "Wait a minute, wait a minute! I'm not ready, I'm not ready!" and they'd cut the cameras.

This went on quite a few times and the two Chucks realized that Cliff was losing his nerve and that he might never give the cue for them to step off the board. They took it upon themselves that the next time, no matter what happened, they were just gonna "adios."

The cameras were rolling and the director yelled, "Action!" Cliff was about to say, "Wait a minute," but the two boys stepped off the board. The horse slid down and there went Cliff and the horse—airborne. They fell a good eighty-five to ninety feet and hit the water. It was a tremendous stunt, but Cliff went looking for the two Chucks because he didn't appreciate the fact that they had just dumped him. But they said if they hadn't, he would never have made the jump.

There was a famous guy who did falls; I think it was Frankie Magraff. The gag (or stunt) on the picture was that Frankie was going to go up on a stone bridge about three hundred feet above this river. The bridge was about four feet high. In the picture business—then as today—when the stuntman has a stunt to do, he goes to the first assistant and they make a deal as to how much it should cost.

Frankie said to the first, "This is dangerous. It's gonna cost you a lotta money. It's gonna cost you a thousand dollars." The assistant said fine.

The cameras were down below by the river and Frankie went up the bank to the stone bridge. Sitting down with their backs against the wall of the stone bridge were two boys about seven or eight years old. The crew couldn't see them from below where the camera was. Frankie got up there and said, "Now, fellas, I'm doing a stunt for this picture we're making and when they tell me, I'm gonna jump off over the side of the bridge here and down into the water. Now, you can stay here, but be sure to stay down because if you stand up, it's gonna ruin the shot." The boys said, "Okay," they would sit there below the edge of the bridge.

The director asked if Frankie was ready and Frankie said, "Fine." The director called "Action!" the cameras were rolling, and there went Frankie over bridge. He fell three hundred feet into the water.

When Frankie came up, two little heads popped up on either side of him. The two kids had jumped right behind him. The first assistant said, "A thousand dollars? Those two little kids did it for free!" Of course, they ruined the shot and Frankie had to go up there and do it again. And this time he didn't let the kids out on the bridge.

The only time I ever got into trouble with stunts was at the end of *The Good Guys and the Bad Guys* when the bad guys are trying to run off with money-filled saddlebags they've taken from a train.

A whole group of townspeople in old-fashioned cars were chasing them, and among the group of cars was a guy riding a 1911 Harley-Davidson motorcycle. The trick was for him to chase one of the bad guys and, when he got close to him, to stand on the seat of the motorcycle and, like they used to do on horseback, dive and catch the bandit.

We had two cameras and they were coming straight at us. I said, "What happens when he jumps off that motorcycle and it keeps coming?" The stunt guy said, "Oh, don't worry. When he jumps, by jumping off, he'll knock the bike over."

I thought, Well, okay, but just in case, the stuntmen got a rope and went out in front of the cameras. One stood on each side of the rope, the plan being that if the motorcycle kept coming, they would catch it in this rope and stop it before it hit the cameras.

We started the shot and the kids started running. The guy on the motorcycle stood up and jumped off. When he jumped off, the motorcycle just kept coming straight as an arrow, right at us. The stunt guys with the rope were afraid to pull the rope up because they were afraid to ruin the shot, even though it was already over. There came the motorcycle and we were all down behind the cameras—the cameraman, the assistants, and me.

The motorcycle came roaring in and at the last moment, the stuntmen tried to catch it in the rope. They missed and it kept coming right into the cameras, now with the rope on it. The rope tangled around the cameras, the cameras fell through their tripod, and the motorcycle was right in among us, still going, round and round in the dirt. Damnedest wreck you ever saw.

Finally, somebody grabbed the kill switch on the motorcycle and got it stopped. We pulled ourselves together and got the cameras back on the tripods. Nobody was hurt and the cameras were fine. I remember in the picture, it was a pretty good shot.

As John Huston said, it's "the Grand Madness." After all, where else but in the picture business would people risk their lives to tell a story that never happened about people who never existed?

17

War Stories

I graduated from high school in 1941 and had planned to attend
Michigan State University, but the war came along. At the time
I was working in Chicago. I went down and I tried to join; they
said it would be three weeks before I could sign up, so I went
back to Muskegon, Michigan, and they put me in right away.

Being a volunteer was a funny thing, as opposed to being
drafted. They lined up the volunteers and a group of the people
who were drafted. To the ones who volunteered, they said, "Hold
up your right hand. Do you swear to uphold the Constitution of
the United States, etc. . . ." And to the guys who enlisted, they
said, "You *do* swear to uphold the Constitution," and that was
really the difference between the volunteers and the draftees.

I was sent to Camp Custer, which was only fitting, because the
reason I joined the Army was that I had seen *They Died with
Their Boots On*, with Errol Flynn, and decided I wanted to be in
the cavalry. I ended up at Camp Custer, and I didn't know anything about the Army.

The first night we got in the barracks, I went to get into my bunk but the sheets were doubled-up, so I had to kick my way to get into bed, which was almost impossible. The next morning I made my bunk, and I did it the way that it was the night before. Somebody said to me, "Whose bunk is that?" I said, "It's mine." They said, "You're short-sheeting it." "Short-sheeting" was a joke that they pulled on new recruits.

The same day I was put on Kitchen Police with another guy. We hadn't done anything wrong, we were just there. We went into a big mess hall, and they put us in the kitchen, where we cleaned big pots and pans all day and all night.

When the Mess Sergeant came in the next morning, he said, "You guys got K.P. two days in a row?"

We said, "No, we've been here all night."

"You only work one day."

"Nobody told us we were through," we said, "so we just stayed here." He felt sorry for us and let us off. We absolutely didn't know anything.

They made me a guide one Sunday, and put a band on my arm that said "Company B Guide." They said, "Now you go out there and stand at the crossroad, and when people come along looking for Company B, you point over here."

I thought, well, I can handle that. I knew there were officers and that you were supposed to salute them, but I didn't know what an officer looked like. So every soldier I saw, I saluted, just to be on the safe side. I saluted privates, corporals—everyone.

I got through that day, and a few more, and was sent to Fort Riley with the horses. I was with the horses about a week. The only thing exciting that happened there was that they fell us out one Sunday and said, "Does anybody here know anything about polo?"

Like an idiot, I put up my hand. They said, "Fall back inside, get your fatigues on, and report to the polo field."

In the cavalry, polo was a big thing, and we had some good players, world-class players. The Army played world-class polo for years. My job in the polo game was to stand at the end line, by the goal, and if somebody hit the ball and it wasn't a goal, I'd have to run and get the ball, put it on the line, and then a horseman would run in behind me, and hit the ball back into play.

These cavalry guys were really rough. When you'd get the ball, they'd start their horse galloping toward you, and you would sometimes barely have enough time to get the ball down before they roared by and hit the ball. It made me realize never to volunteer for anything in the Army again—and I never did.

When I was in Fort Riley, I decided that I wanted to be an officer. I had passed the test with enough points. They took a bunch of us who had qualified, and put us in a six-by-six truck with our barracks bags. The last thing we had to do was take a physical before we shipped out. We were all going to tank destroyer school.

I took my physical, and everything was fine until the eye test. I failed it. They threw my barracks bag off the truck and pulled out of Officers' School. When they did my test, they gave me some eye drops, and I was blind. I couldn't see a thing, and I had to find my way back to my old outfit.

Somehow, I managed to get on a bus, and people were kind enough to show me back to my troop area. I was a squad leader, and in my squad was Oleg Cassini, who was married to Jean Tierney. Jean came to visit, and I let Oleg have my pass so he could stay off the post with Tierney for one or two nights. Then they moved her into the officers' quarters. She stayed the rest of the week on the post.

She was a fantastic girl, and I was only nineteen so I was really star-struck. One day she had a sore throat, and she wanted to know if I would take her over to the infirmary so they could do something for her.

I got her in a Jeep and took her to the infirmary. When I went in, I said, "I've got Jean Tierney here," and they all went, "Oh, sure . . ." She came in, and they were all flabbergasted.

✵ ✵ ✵ ✵ ✵

Speaking of infirmaries, one of my first duties when I became what they called an Officer Candidate was to fall in the whole troop of two hundred guys. The officer handed me a list of names and said, "Now Kennedy, take these people over to the infirmary, and get their shots. They're all lined up alphabetically. Just march them over there, get them their shots, and march them back."

I thought—okay, I can do this. But the problem was, I didn't read the order, and the place where we'd always gotten our shots was clear across camp, at Infirmary Three. I didn't realize we were supposed to go to Infirmary Number Two.

I had them all in line, marching them in columns of twos to the other end of the camp, when I suddenly realized that they weren't supposed to go to this infirmary, that they're supposed to go the infirmary that was right across the street from our area. I panicked and halted the group. Now, there were two hundred of them. And I said, "About face."

They had been in alphabetical order, and now the "Z's" are up front, and the "A's" are at the end of the line. Then, to make matters worse, I started to double-time because I was late. As they double-timed, a lot of them fell behind. Now the "Z's" were falling back into the "S's" and the "T's" . . . it was a complete mess.

I finally got them to the right infirmary, which was about a hundred yards from where we'd started. If I had been officer material before, I sure as hell wasn't anymore. I went into the infirmary, and the captain who was in charge was sitting behind his desk. I started to explain how I screwed up. He had an open bottle of black ink on his desk, and I reached over and spilled it all over his desk and all over him. He looked up and saw the shape I was in, and he said, "Just sit down over there and we'll take care of it. Don't worry about anything. It's no problem; we'll do it."

They all got their shots, and I marched them back the hundred yards to the troop area. I reported to the commander, "Mission accomplished." He never knew the difference.

I stayed in Riley for about six months, and then I transferred to the First Cavalry Division in Fort Bliss, Texas. We had horses for about four months, and then they took our horses away and made us infantry. Soon after that, we were shipped out to San Francisco, where we got on a boat and went to Australia.

In Australia, enough time had gone by so I could apply for Officers' School again, and this time I passed. I was sent to an infantry school called Camp Columbia in Brisbane. At Officers' School, we started with about 850 candidates, and 250 graduated. It was really a tough school. It was tough because when you graduated, they'd send you right up north to New Guinea, and some of the graduates were killed forty-eight hours after they got their commissions, so they had to be careful who they put up there.

❊   ❊   ❊   ❊   ❊

When I was in Fort Bliss, they put me on guard duty. They gave you a rifle and said, "Now you walk around this block, and just keep walking until somebody stops you and takes over." I think we walked two hours at a time.

I started to walk, carrying a rifle, and I got up to the PX, and there was an officer who came by me, and he stopped and said, "Soldier, don't you know you have to salute an officer?"

I really didn't—carrying a rifle.

So he said, "Come to port arms." I didn't know what "port arms" was, so I just took the rifle off my shoulder and stood there. He bawled the hell out of me.

About two weeks later, I was assigned duty at an officers' dance at Fort Bliss. The officers, who were always trying to hang on to tradition, wore their dress uniforms, capes, and sabers. The capes had yellow silk linings. They had dancing spurs, which are spurs which have small rouls on them so that they don't kick the ladies.

I was assigned to this party as a bus boy. I had to wear a little white jacket. My job was to go around pouring coffee for the officers. I did all right for quite a while, and then there was this officer who called me over for some coffee, and when I poured it, I spilled it on him.

As you might know, it was the same officer who had stopped me out in front of the PX and bawled the hell out of me. His name was Lt. Snow. And his problem, which I found out years later, was that he was passed up in rank, and in the regular Army, when it came time to get promoted, he didn't. So he was very bitter.

I should skip forward to when we were in Manila. The Manila campaign was over, and we had our headquarters at the Wackwack Golf Course. One day, I was going into the headquarters, and there were about five officers who were just joining the outfit.

We never wore any insignia when we were in the field, because the Japanese used to like to shoot officers. I didn't have any insignia on, and I was walking up to the front of the headquarters building at Wackwack. This prissy officer stopped me, and made me stand at attention, and he wanted to know all about the First Cavalry Division.

Now, I'd been through the whole war, and by this time, I was pretty tough, but I just let him go ahead, and I said, "Yes, sir, yes, sir . . ."

One of those new officers was Lt. Snow, the officer who had given me the hard time back at Fort Bliss. That night we were having dinner. Whenever possible, we would have what they call an Officers' Mess. It had a table and chairs, and the officers would sit down to eat. At the head of the table was the troop commander, which at that time was me.

Two of those new officers who had stopped me in front of the headquarters were assigned to my troop, and one of them was Lt. Snow.

The officers couldn't sit down to the table until the troop commander came in and sat. It was all a bunch of baloney, but they stuck to it. So I came in, and they were all standing there waiting, and I sat down at the head of the table. Lt. Snow saw me and turned white because he was sure that somehow I'd get even with him.

As it turns out, I never did. He was always waiting for the other shoe to fall. The officer who came with him was killed the very next day.

My first assignment after Officers' School was in the Admiralty Islands. I reported to a Colonel Lowe. I was young, and he resented that. I recall him telling me that no matter how bad things got, in the Army or in life, something would always happen to turn things around. I didn't pay any attention to him, but I kept running into him, like on Sundays, when we would play volleyball. I wasn't a volleyball player, but I used to play basketball, so I sort of understand it. About three or four times during the game, I was playing the net and spiked the ball right in the colonel's face, which didn't help matters.

Then we had a dress parade. I had been assigned to H Troop, a heavy weapons outfit, and I was in charge of a section of water-cooled machine guns.

I was out in front of my section. Everybody was wearing steel helmets. I just wore the helmet liner, because it was lighter. The colonel, who was reviewing the troops saw me and bawled the hell out of me. "Why are you wearing a helmet liner? What kind of a soldier are you?" He really gave it to me.

The following weekend, a hospital ship was in the bay called "The Hope." The nurses would come in to our island, and a party would be held for them at the Officers' Club. I went to this party, and there was this real good-looking nurse. I started hitting on her. You didn't call it that in 1942, but that's what I was doing. Well, it turned out she was Colonel Lowe's girlfriend. I didn't know it, but by this time he was ready to kill me.

Things went along and we finally shipped out of there. We made a landing: the Leyte Invasion. During the Leyte Invasion, this colonel just kept after me. One day we were marching some-where. I'd found a little kid who was about seven years old, and he wanted to wear my helmet. I let him wear the helmet, and we were walking along, and he was right behind me.

This colonel came up and he said, "No helmet again." He said, "Put your helmet on!" Oh, by the way . . . I was *not* wearing a helmet liner, I was wearing the little kid's straw hat, which was not too smart. He bawled the hell out of me again. He said, "At least look like a soldier."

On the first morning after the landing, we got into a tight spot. I had the machine guns, and the machine guns in a heavy weapons company always brought up the rear. If something happened up front, they'd call me up with the guns.

There was a sniper. We got the guns in, and this guy started shooting at us, and Colonel Lowe hit the ground right alongside of me. He had a camera around his neck attached to a leather strap. The sniper shot at him and missed, but he hit the camera into the ground. It busted the camera, and the colonel got up and ran.

Just as he got up, he caught my eye. It was like I caught him. Now, he was a big hero. He'd been awarded the Distinguished Service Cross, the Silver Star, and a few other things . . . but he ran, and I saw him, and that didn't help matters either.

We were moving into a town called Barrugo. There was a main street that went right down to the water's edge, and out into the bay, the South China Sea. This is where they put our guns—one machine gun on one side of the road, and one on the other.

The crews dug the guns in, and then someone in the mortar outfit decided that they were going to zero in on some targets just before it got dark. This is so that if there's an attack during the night and they can't see, they've already zeroed in targets that the Japanese could hide behind. They zero in on these spots, and then they set their guns at a certain setting so that in the dark, if we were attacked, they could just put the gun at a certain setting and drop mortars right on top of these hiding places.

At dusk, they decided to zero in these 81mm mortars up the beach from us, to our left, on some possible targets. No one had told the citizenry of the village, so when mortars started exploding, they all panicked, with one guy running down the beach and yelling, "The Japs are coming!"

I decided to move the one machine gun across the road and put it in alongside the other machine gun, pointing them up the beach. This is where the mortars were apparently coming from.

When one of the gun crew went to move the gun, he accidentally hit the trigger, and it fired about five rounds out into the water.

This gunfire, added to the mortar fire, made everybody *really* panic. Now people were running up and down the street and all hell was breaking loose. All of a sudden, Colonel Lowe came running up to the guns and said, "Who fired that gun?"

I said, "I did." One of the section sergeants said, "No he didn't—the gunner did." The colonel was so mad that he just

hauled off and hit me, knocked me to my knees. I was wearing a
.45, and I pulled it out. I was going to kill the sonofabitch, but
the Sergeant grabbed him, and everything calmed down. By then
he knew he had done the wrong thing. He was saying to me,
"Look, I only did that to show the men how serious this was. It
didn't mean anything. I hit you, but I didn't mean it."

We got that under control, and the next day in Barrugo I was
in a chow line in town. We used to wear coveralls. They were a
pain in the neck, because when you had to go to the latrine, you
had to take the whole thing down in order to go. There was a
belt right around the middle of it though, so I got the bright idea
of cutting it off—to make it a jacket. So I cut it off all the way
around, above the belt. I was in this chow line, and the colonel
saw me, and he said, "What happened to your uniform?"

I said, "It ripped off."

He looked at me and he said, "You, above everybody in the
Army, have the priority to get a new uniform. Go to the quartermaster and get a new uniform." So I finished eating, and I went
to the quartermaster, and I got a new uniform.

The next day, Captain Thorne, who was our troop commander,
came to me and said, "Burt, I want to tell you something. Last
night, we were sleeping in this house in town, and Colonel Lowe
woke me up in the middle of the night, and he said, 'Do you
think a pair of coveralls could rip off that way so cleanly, or do
you think they were cut?' " Thorne, who had seen him ragging
on me for almost two years, said to me, "Burt, I think he's going
crazy." He said, "Just watch him. Don't let him get behind you.
There's something wrong with him. Just watch yourself."

I said okay, because I thought he was crazy, too.

After we made our landing in Luzon we ended up going to
Manila and then later on down to Lucina Tiabas, where we had
our final camp. I hadn't seen Colonel Lowe around. Captain
Thorne said, "Well, he's been transferred. They think he's beginning to crack. Because he's a war hero, they don't want to put too
much pressure on him, so they transferred him to G-2, Intelli-
gence."

I was told, about three months later, just before the war ended, that the colonel was in a rear echelon. In the middle of the night, he had to go to the latrine. When you were in the field, they used to cut what they called "slit trenches." They were about two feet wide, six feet deep, and if you had to go, you just squatted down over the slit trench and went.

He was out there in the middle of the night, the war was still on, and he squatted down over the slit trench. They had a war dog in the area, and the Colonel didn't know that he was chained. So here comes this war dog to attack the colonel. He got right to him before his chain pulled him back, and the colonel panicked and fell over backward, and he fell into this slit trench, with a lot of doo-doo.

He was wedged down in there, and it was so narrow that he couldn't move. He yelled and hollered, and they came and got him out. As I was told, they put him in a straitjacket and took him to the booby pen. He got a Section Eight—and he was gone.

When I heard that he was gone, I remember that when I first met him, he told me about when things got so bad you didn't think you could take it, something always happened to change things. He was right.

After the war I heard that he had since recovered.

18

My Star

When the western began to fade, I turned to television and did a number of shows. Two hours, five hours, six hours—all kinds of shows, mostly with horses in them.

Speaking of horses, a horse was the only star I ever discovered in my fifty years in the business. We were preparing to make *The Rounders* and we needed a little, cantankerous roan horse that Glenn Ford battles all through the picture. We went out to Fat Jones Stables, a stable where many horses in the picture business were kept.

We looked around and I spotted this little horse. He was perfect. But Fat Jones said, "You can't use him; he's a three-year-old. He's never seen a camera and he'll give you nothing but trouble."

I was very disappointed, but I kept my eye on him because he looked perfect for the part. The horses had to put a lot of tricks on and there were no roans available which could be trained.

Someone got the bright idea to take two Appaloosa horses with a little roan color in them and dye them the roan color.

I said, "Can you do that?" One of the hands assured me, "Oh, yeah, sure. We'll just dye 'em and make 'em roans."

About two weeks later, I got a call to go out to the stable to take a look at my new roans. The problem was, when the horses were dyed, instead of being roan horses, they were streaked, almost like zebras, with purple stripes all over them. I said, "What are we going to do?"

The answer was, "Well, it'll take three months for the hair to grow out so we can clip them and start over."

I snapped, "Start over, hell. Get me the little horse I looked at before!"

They brought out the little roan horse, his original name was Pye, I believe. In the picture he was called Ol' Fooler. From then on, he was Ol' Fooler.

After *The Rounders*, in which he was very good although he was a problem at first, he settled down and he became a big star. Burt Lancaster rode him in *The Scalp Hunters* and did some comedy tricks with him. Robert Redford rode him in *Jeremiah Johnson*. He worked all the time.

Many years later, I had him in a *Simon & Simon* episode for television. He was getting old but he was still just great.

A few years down the road, I was attending a music scoring of a picture I had done at the old Republic lot, which is now CBS. During one of the breaks, I walked out the side door of the stage and I looked over to see about ten horses tied to a horse truck off to one side, in the shade. A western was being filmed on the back lot. I looked along the line of horses and there was my star, Ol' Fooler, with his head down.

I went over and I talked to him. He kind of nickered a little— he knew me. He was then twenty-three or twenty-four. And I felt this terrible sadness. He had been used until he was too old to really do all of his wonderful tricks, and he had just been tied to a truck.

About five years later, I heard a wonderful horse trainer had bought him and had turned him loose in a pasture to run. He did that until the day he died two years ago. Ol' Fooler, the only star I ever discovered.

*   *   *   *   *

There was an old saying in Vaudeville: "When your act is over, be sure you don't get hit on the head when the curtain is coming down."

My act is over, so I'll get off before I get hit in the head or somebody ties me to a horse-truck.

*   *   *   *   *

That's a wrap.

Filmography

1956   **Seven Men from Now** (Batjac-Warner Bros.)—Directed
        by Budd Boetticher. Produced by Andrew V. McLaglen,
        Robert E. Morrison. Camera (WarnerColor), William
        Clothier. Music, Henry Vars. CAST: Randolph Scott, Gail
        Russell, Lee Marvin, Walter Reed, Donald Barry, John
        Larch, Fred Graham, Chuck Roberson, Stuart Whitman.

1956   **Man in the Vault** (RKO)—Directed by Andrew V.
        McLaglen. Produced by Robert E. Morrison. Camera
        (B&W), William Clothier. Music, Henry Vars. Based on
        the novel *The Lock and the Key,* by Frank Gruber. CAST:
        William Campbell, Karen Sharpe, Anita Ekberg, Berry
        Kroeger, Paul Fix, Mike Mazurki, Gonzales Gonzales.

1957   **Gun the Man Down** (UA)—Directed by Andrew V. McLaglen. Produced by Robert E. Morrison. Camera (B&W), William Clothier. Music, Henry Vars. Based on a story by Sam C. Freedle. CAST: James Arness, Angie Dickinson, Robert J. Wilke, Emile Meyer, Don Megowan, Harry Carey Jr.

1957   **The Tall T** (Columbia)—Directed by Budd Boetticher. A Scott-Brown Production, produced by Harry Joe Brown. Camera (Technicolor), Charles Lawton. Music, Heinz Roemheld. Based on a story by Elmore Leonard. CAST: Randolph Scott, Richard Boone, Maureen O'Sullivan, Arthur Hunnicutt, Skip Homeier, Henry Silva, John Hubbard.

1958   **Fort Dobbs** (Warner Bros.)—Coscreenplay with George W. George. Directed by Gordon Douglas. Produced by Martin Rackin. Camera (B&W), William Clothier. Music, Max Steiner. CAST: Clint Walker, Virginia Mayo, Brian Keith, Richard Eyer, Michael Dante.

1958   **Buchanan Rides Alone** (Columbia)—Coscreenplay (uncredited) with Charles Lang. Directed by Budd Boetticher. Produced by Harry Joe Brown. Camera (ColumbiaColor), Lucien Ballard. Based on the novel *The Name's Buchanan,* by Jonas Ward. CAST: Randolph Scott, Craig Stevens, Barry Kelley, L. Q. Jones, Peter Whitney, William Leslie, Jennifer Holden, Roy Jenson, Joe De Santis.

1959   **Ride Lonesome** (Columbia)—Directed by Budd Boetticher. A Scott-Brown Production, produced by Harry Joe Brown. Camera (CinemaScope-Color), Charles Lawton. Music, Heinz Roemheld. CAST: Randolph Scott, Karen Steele, Pernell Roberts, James Best, James Coburn, Lee Van Cleef.

1959   **Yellowstone Kelly** (Warner Bros.)—Directed by Gordon Douglas. No producer credited. Camera (Technicolor), Carl Guthrie. Music, Howard Jackson. Based on a novel by Clay Fisher (Will Henry). CAST: Clint Walker, Andrea Martin, Edd Byrnes, John Russell, Ray Danton, Claude Akins, Warren Oates.

1960   **Comanche Station** (Columbia)—Directed by Budd Boetticher. A Scott-Brown Production, produced by Harry Joe Brown. Camera (CinemaScope-Eastman Color), Charles Lawton. Music, Heinz Roemheld. CAST: Randolph Scott, Nancy Gates, Claude Akins, Richard Rust, Skip Homeier, Rand Brooks.

1962   **Six Black Horses** (Universal)—Directed by Harry Keller. Produced by Gordon Kay. Camera (Color), Maury Gertsman. CAST: Audie Murphy, Dan Duryea, Joan O'Brien, Bob Steele, Roy Barcroft.

1966   **Return of the Gunfighter** (MGM)—Coscreenplay with Robert Buckner. Directed by James Neilson. Produced by Frank and Maurice King. CAST: Robert Taylor, Chad Everett, Anna Martin, Michael Pate, Lyle Bettger, John Davis Chandler.

1968   **Stay Away, Joe** (MGM)—Coscreenplay (uncredited) with Michael Hoey. Directed by Peter Tewksbury. Produced by Douglas Lawrence. CAST: Elvis Presley, Katy Jurado, Burgess Meredith, Joan Blondell, Thomas Gomez, L. Q. Jones.

1977   **The Littlest Horse Thieves** (aka Escape from the Dark) (Walt Disney-Buena Vista)—Story by Burt Kennedy and Rosemary Anne Sisson; screenplay by Sisson. Directed by Charles Jarrott. Produced by Ron Miller. CAST: Alastair Sim, Andrew Harrison, Benjie Bolgar, Chloe Franks.

1990   **White Hunter, Black Heart** (Warner Bros.)—Directed by Clint Eastwood. Produced by Clint Eastwood, David Valdes, Stanley Rubin. Coscreenplay with Peter Viertel, James Bridges. Based on the novel by Viertel. CAST: Clint Eastwood, Jeff Fahey, George Dzundza, Marisa Berenson.

Direction

1960   **The Canadians** (20th-Fox)—Also screenplay. Produced by Herman E. Webber. Camera (CinemaScope-DeLuxe Color), Arthur Ibbetson. CAST: Robert Ryan, John Dehner, Torin Thatcher, John Sutton, Michael Pate.

1962   **The Lawman** (Warner Bros. Television)—Half-hour B&W western series. Produced by Jules Schermer. Executive producer, William T. Orr. STARS: John Russell, Peter Brown, Peggie Castle.

Kennedy directed four episodes:
"The Long Gun"—Also teleplay. With John Dehner.
"Sunday"—Also teleplay. With Andrew Duggan.
"The Wanted Man"—Also teleplay. With Marie Windsor.
"Cort"

1962   **The Virginian** (Revue-MCA)—Ninety-minute western series derived from the Owen Wister novel. Executive Producer, Norman MacDonnell. Produced by Howard Christie, Paul Freeman, Jim McAdams. STARS: James Drury, Lee J. Cobb, Doug McClure, Pippa Scott, Gary Clarke, Roberta Shore.

Kennedy wrote and directed one episode: "The Woman From White Wing"—with Barry Sullivan.

1962   **Combat** (ABC-Selmur Productions)—One-hour World War II combat series. STARS: Rick Jason, Vic Morrow, Pierre Jalbert, Steve Rogers, Shecky Greene.

Kennedy wrote and directed three first-season episodes:
"Lost Sheep, Lost Shepherd"—With Jeffrey Hunter.
"Next in Command"—With Ben Cooper.
"The Walking Wounded"—With Gary Merrill, Geraldine Brooks.

1963   **Mail Order Bride** (UK: West of Montana) (MGM)—Also screenplay. Produced by Richard E. Lyons. Camera (Panavision-MetroColor), Paul C. Vogel. CAST: Buddy Ebsen, Keir Dullea, Lois Nettleton, Warren Oates, Marie Windsor, Paul Fix, Barbara Luna.

1965   **The Rounders** (MGM)—Also screenplay, from the novel by Max Evans. Produced by Richard E. Lyons. Camera (Panavision-MetroColor), Paul C. Vogel. Music, Jeff Alexander. CAST: Glenn Ford, Henry Fonda, Chill Wills, Sue Ane Langdon, Hope Holiday, Edgar Buchanan, Joan Freeman, Warren Oates.

1966   **The Money Trap** (MGM)—Screenplay by Walter Bernstein, from the novel by Lionel White. Produced by Max Youngstein, David Karr. Camera (B&W Panavision), Paul C. Vogel. Music, Hal Schaefer. CAST: Glenn Ford, Elke Sommer, Rita Hayworth, Ricardo Montalban, Joseph Cotten, Tom Reese, Jim Mitchum.

1966   **Return of the Seven** (Mirisch-UA)—Screenplay by Larry Cohen. Produced by Ted Richmond. Camera (Panavision-Color), Paul C. Vogel. Sequel to *The Magnificent Seven* (1961). Music, Elmer Bernstein. CAST: Yul Brynner, Robert Fuller, Warren Oates, Claude Akins, Emilio Fernandez, Rodolfo Acosta, Fernando Rey.

1967   **Welcome to Hard Times** (MGM)—Also screenplay, from the novel by E. L. Doctorow. Produced by Max Youngstein, David Karr. Camera (MetroColor), Harry Stradling Jr. Music, Harry Sukman. CAST: Henry Fonda,

Janice Rule, Aldo Ray, Keenan Wynn, Janis Paige, John Anderson, Warren Oates, Fay Spain, Edgar Buchanan, Denver Pyle, Lon Chaney, Royal Dano, Paul Birch, Paul Fix, Elisha Cook.

1967   **The War Wagon** (Batjac-Universal)—Screenplay by Clair Huffaker, from the novel by Marvin H. Albert. Produced by Marvin Schwartz. Camera (Panavision, Technicolor), William Clothier. Music, Dimitri Tiomkin. CAST: John Wayne, Kirk Douglas, Howard Keel, Robert Walker, Keenan Wynn, Bruce Cabot, Joanna Barnes, Gene Evans.

1969   **Support Your Local Sheriff** (UA)—Screenplay by William Bowers. Produced by Bowers for Cherokee Productions (James Garner). Camera (DeLuxe Color), Harry Stradling Jr. CAST: James Garner, Joan Hackett, Walter Brennan, Harry Morgan, Henry Jones, Jack Elam, Bruce Dern, Gene Evans, Willis Bouchey.

1969   **Young Billy Young** (UA)—Also screenplay, from the novel *Who Rides with Wyatt,* by Will Henry. Produced by Max Youngstein. Camera (DeLuxe Color), Harry Stradling Jr. Music, Shelley Manne. Title song sung by Robert Mitchum. CAST: Robert Mitchum, Angie Dickinson, Robert Walker, David Carradine, Jack Kelly, John Anderson, Paul Fix, Willis Bouchey, Rodolfo Acosta.

1969   **The Good Guys and The Bad Guys** (Warner Bros.-7 Arts)—Screenplay by Ronald M. Cohen and Dennis Shryack. Produced by Cohen and Shryack. Executive producer, Robert Goldstein. Camera (Panavision, Technicolor), Harry Stradling Jr. Music, William Lava. CAST: Robert Mitchum, George Kennedy, Tina Louise, David Carradine, John Carradine, Lois Nettleton, Martin Balsam, Douglas V. Fowley, John Davis Chandler, Marie Windsor, Kathleen Freeman, Nick Dennis.

1970   **Dirty Dingus Magee** (MGM)—Screenplay by Tom and Frank Waldman and Joseph Heller. Produced by Burt Kennedy. Camera (Panavision, Metrocolor), Harry Stradling Jr. Music, Jeff Alexander. Based on the novel by David Markson. CAST: Frank Sinatra, George Kennedy, Lois Nettleton, Anne Jackson, Jack Elam, John Dehner, Henry Jones, Harry Carey Jr., Paul Fix, Michele Carey.

1971   **The Deserter** (De Laurentiis-Paramount)—Screenplay by Clair Huffaker. Produced for Dino De Laurentiis by Norman Baer and Ralph Serpe. Camera (Panavision, Technicolor), Aldo Tonti. CAST: Bekim Fehmiu, John Huston, Richard Cenna, Ricardo Montalban, Chuck Connors, Ian Bannen, Brandon de Wilde, Slim Pickens, Woody Strode, Patrick Wayne, Albert Salmi.

1971   **Support Your Local Gunfighter** (UA)—Screenplay by James Edward Grant. Produced by Bill Finnegan. Executive producer, Burt Kennedy. Camera (DeLuxe Color), Harry Stradling Jr. CAST: James Garner, Suzanne Pleshette, Jack Elam, Joan Blondell, Harry Morgan, Marie Windsor, Henry Jones, John Dehner, Dub Taylor, Chuck Connors, Dick Curtis, Grady Sutton.

1972   **Hannie Caulder** (Paramount)—Also coscreenplay with David Raft (under the combined pseudonym Z. X. Jones). Produced by Patrick Curtis. Camera (Panavision, Technicolor), Edward "Ted" Scaife. Music, Ken Thorne. CAST: Raquel Welch, Robert Culp, Ernest Borgnine, Strother Martin, Jack Elam, Christopher Lee, Diana Dors.

1973   **The Train Robbers** (Batjac-Warner Bros.)—Also screenplay. Produced for Batjac by Michael Wayne. Camera (Panavision, Technicolor), William Clothier. Music, Dominic Frontiere. CAST: John Wayne, Ann-Margret, Rod

Taylor, Ben Johnson, Ricardo Montalban, Bobby Vinton, Christopher George.

1974 **Shootout in a One-Dog Town** (TVM; ABC-Hanna-Barbera)—Teleplay by Dick Nelson and Larry Cohen, from a story by Larry Cohen. Produced for Hanna-Barbera by Richard E. Lyons. Camera, Robert B. Hauser. CAST: Richard Crenna, Stefanie Powers, Jack Elam, Richard Egan, Arthur O'Connell, Michael Ansara, Bud Taylor, Gene Evans, Michael Anderson Jr.

1974 **Sidekicks** (TVM; Warner Bros. TV)—Teleplay by William Bowers, based on characters created by Richard Alan Simmons (*The Skin Game*). Produced by Burt Kennedy. Camera, Robert B. Hauser. Music, David Shire. CAST: Larry Hagman, Louis Gossett Jr., Blythe Danner, Jack Elam, Harry Morgan, Gene Evans, Noah Beery Jr., Denver Pyle, John Beck.

1974 **All the Kind Strangers** (TVM; Cinemation)—Teleplay by Clyde Ware. Produced for Cinemation by Roger Lewis. Camera, Robert B. Hauser, Gene Polito. Music, Ron Frangipane. Songs performed by Robby Benson. CAST: Stacy Keach, Samantha Eggar, John Savage, Robby Benson.

1976 **The Killer Inside Me** (Warner Bros.)—Screenplay by Edward Mann and Robert Chamblee, from the novel by Jim Thompson. Producers, Irving Cohen, Michael W. Leighton. Camera (Panavision, Color), William A. Fraker. Music, Tim McIntire, John Rubinstein. CAST: Stacy Keach, Susan Tyrrell, Tisha Sterling, Keenan Wynn, John Dehner, Don Stroud, Julie Adams, Royal Dano, Charles McGraw, John Carradine.

1976 **Drum** (De Laurentiis-UA)—Replaced as director by Steve Carver. Screenplay by Norman Wexler, from a novel by Kyle Onstott. Produced for De Laurentiis by

Ralph Serpe. Camera (Color), Lucien Ballard. CAST: Warren Oates, Isela Vega, Ken Norton, Pam Grier, Yaphet Kotto, John Colicos, Fiona Lewis, Royal Dano, Paula Kelly, Harvey Parry.

1977 **Big Hawaii** (UK: Danger in Paradise)—One-hour color television drama series. Created by William Woods. Produced for CBS/Filmways by Perry Lafferty. STARS: John Dehner, Cliff Potts, Bill Lucking.

Kennedy directed two episodes of this series: "Yesterdays,"—with Jack Starrett and Michael Parks, and "Pipeline."

1977 **How the West Was Won** (MGM-TV)—Six-hour miniseries for ABC, telecast in three two-hour segments. Developed for television by Albert S. Ruddy and Jim Byrnes, based on the telefeature *The Macahans,* and the movie *How the West Was Won.* Executive producer, John Mantley. Codirected by Kennedy and Daniel Mann. CAST: James Arness, Eva Marie Saint, Bruce Boxleitner, Anthony Zerbe, Don Murray, Kathryn Holcomb, Jack Elam, John Dehner, Royal Dano, David Huddleston, Paul Fix.

1977 **The Rhineman Exchange** (Universal-TV)—Five-hour miniseries for NBC, shown in three parts; subsequently cut by one hour and shown in two parts. Teleplay by Richard Collins, from the novel by Robert Ludlum. Producers, George Eckstein, Collins. Camera, Alex Phillips Jr. Music, Elmer Bernstein, Michel Colombier. CAST: Stephen Collins, Lauren Hutton, Claude Akins, Vince Edwards, Jose Ferrer, Larry Hagman, John Huston, Roddy McDowall, Gene Evans, Jeremy Kemp, Werner Klemperer, Isela Vega, Victoria Racimo, Pedro Armendariz Jr., Rene Auberjonois, John Hoyt.

1978 **Kate Bliss and the Ticker-Tape Kid** (TVM; Aaron Spelling)—Teleplay by William Bowers. Produced for Spelling by Richard E. Lyons. Camera, Lamar Boren. Music, Jeff Alexander. CAST: Suzanne Pleshette, Don Meredith, Harry Morgan, David Huddleston, Tony Randall, Burgess Meredith, Buck Taylor, Gene Evans, Harry Carey Jr., Don "Red" Barry, Alvy Moore, John Hart.

1979   **The Wild Wild West Revisited** (TVM; CBS Entertainment)—Teleplay by William Bowers, based on the series produced by Fred Freiberger and John Mantley. Producers, Jay Bernstein and Robert L. Jacks. Camera, Robert B. Hauser. Music, Jeff Alexander. CAST: Robert Conrad, Ross Martin, Paul Williams, Harry Morgan, Rene Auberjonois, Trisha Noble, Jo Ann Harris, Wilford Brimley, Skip Homeier, Joyce Jameson.

1979   **The Concrete Cowboys** (TVM)—Teleplay by Jimmy Sangster. Executive producer, Ernie Frankel. Camera, Alan Stensvold. Music, Earle Hagen. CAST: Jerry Reed, Tom Selleck, Morgan Fairchild, Claude Akins, Lucille Benson, Gene Evans and, as themselves, Roy Acuff, Barbara Mandrell, Ray Stevens.

1980   **More Wild Wild West** (TVM; CBS Entertainment)— Teleplay by Tony Kayden and Williams Bowers, from a story by William Bowers. Producers, Jay Bernstein, Robert L. Jacks. Camera, Charles G. Arnold. Music, Jeff Alexander. CAST: Robert Conrad, Ross Martin, Jonathan Winters, Harry Morgan, Rene Auberjonois, Victor Buono, Emma Samms, Liz Torres, Jack LaLanne, Dr. Joyce Brothers, James Bacon, Avery Schreiber, Casey Tibbs.

1981   **Wolf Lake** (aka The Honor Guard; finished in 1978) Also screenplay. No other information known. May not have received theatrical release in U.S. CAST: Rod Steiger, David Huffman, Robin Mattson, Jerry Hardin, Richard Herd, Paul Mantee.

1987   **The Alamo: 13 Days to Glory** (TVM)—Teleplay by Nor-
        man Morrill and Clyde Ware, from the nonfiction book
        by J. Lon Tinkle. Produced by Stockton Briggle, Bill Fin-
        negan, Pat Finnegan. No other information known.
        CAST: James Arness (Jim Bowie), Alec Baldwin (Colonel
        Travis), Brian Keith (Davy Crockett), Raul Julia (Santa
        Anna), Lorne Greene (Sam Houston), Isela Vega, Gene
        Evans, Ethan Wayne. (Battle scenes filmed by John El-
        senbach.)

1987   **Down The Long Hills** (TVM; Walt Disney)—Produced
        by The Finnegan Company (Bill Finnegan) for Disney.
        No other information known. CAST: Bruce Boxleitner,
        Jack Elam, Bo Hopkins, Thomas Wilson Brown, Lisa
        MacFarlane.